2 vol. 청소년 영어성경공부 교재

We Want to Be Real Christians!

kmc

이현주

감리교신학대학교 영어담당 교수

이화여자대학교 영문학과를 졸업하고 동대학원에서 영문학 석 · 박사학위와 Wesley Theological Seminary에서 목회학 박사 학위를 받았다. 사립학교 영어교사 자격증을 소유하고 있으며, 미국 Teachers College Columbia University에서 TESOL Certificate도 취득했다.

저서로는 『자, 이제 제대로 된 영어를 하자』, 『영작문 한 권으로 따라잡기』, 『난생 처음 쓰는 영어일기: 초급편』, 『난생 처음 쓰는 영어일기: 직장인편』, 『논리가 살아나는 영어 에세이 쓰기』, 『1% 더 실천하는 엄마가 영어 영재 만든다』, 『영어로 신학 맛보기』, 『초기 개신교 선교사의 시와 헌신: 그 부르심의 길』 등이 있으며, 『아서 왕의 죽음 1, 2』, 『이화』를 비롯한 많은 역서가 있다.

We Want to Be Real Christians! Vol. 2

펴낸날 | 2016년 3월 30일

펴낸이 | 전용재

엮은곳 | 기독교대한감리회 교육국
www.kmcedu.or.kr

엮은이 | 김낙환

지은이 | 이현주

그린이 | 최정을

디자인 | 조영라

펴낸곳 | 기독교대한감리회 출판국 · 도서출판 kmc
한만철
서울시 종로구 세종대로 149 감리회관 16층
TEL. 02-399-2008 FAX. 02-399-2085
www.kmcmall.co.kr
methpub@chol.com

등 록 | 제2-1607호 (1993. 9. 4)

인 쇄 | 우일인쇄공사

ISBN 978-89-8430-703-2 04230
978-89-8430 626 4 04230 (세트)

값 7,000원

▶ 이 도서의 국립중앙도서관 출판예정도서목록(CIP)은 서지정보유통지원시스템 홈페이지(http://seoji.nl.go.kr)와 국가자료공동목록시스템(http://www.nl.go.kr/kolisnet)에서 이용하실 수 있습니다. (CIP제어번호: CIP2016005360)

My heart rejoices in the LORD;

. . .

There is no one holy like the LORD;

there is no one besides you;

there is no Rock like our God.

(1 Samuel 2:1-2)

Preface

이 책은 하나님 말씀을 영어로 배우는 책입니다!

감리교신학대학교의 영어 교수로 재직하면서 제가 꼭 해보고 싶었고 또 소명이라 믿었던 일은 영어성경학교 교재 개발이었습니다. 『자, 이제 제대로 된 영어를 하자』(평민사), 『영작문 한 권으로 따라잡기』(다락원), 『난생 처음 쓰는 영어일기』 초급편, 직장인편(넥서스), 『논리가 살아나는 영어 에세이 쓰기』(넥서스), 『영어로 신학 맛보기』(신앙과 지성사) 등 영어 교재를 계속 집필하면서 영어성경학교 교재를 함께 개발하려 하였지만 원하는 결과를 얻지 못하였습니다. 여러 번 시도하였지만 계속 이뤄지지 않는 상황을 접하면서 영어성경학교 교재 개발은 저의 소명이 아니라 생각하고 포기했습니다. 그러나 이와 같은 저의 생각은 Wesley Theological Seminary에서 목회학 박사 과정을 공부하면서 변화하기 시작했습니다.

제 목회학 박사 논문 제목은 *An Intensive English Bible School Program for Under Privileged Children at Sae-Onyang Church*입니다. 논문 준비를 위해 실제 교회 현장에서 영어 프로그램을 운영해보며 현장의 소리를 듣게 되었습니다. 미자립 교회나 지방의 교회에서 영어로 된 프로그램에 대한 요구의 소리를 들었습니다. 또 경제적, 사회적 환경 때문에 영어 교육을 따로 받지 못하는 아이들의 모습도 보았습니다. 영어성경학교 교재를 개발하는 것이 이들 교회와 아이들에게 조금이나마 도움이 되지 않을까 하는 생각이 다시 들었습니다.

목회학 박사 과정은 제게 영어성경교재 개발의 방법론을 일깨워 주었습니다. 제가 집필한 일련의 영어 관련 서적들은 대부분 어떻게 하면 영어 능력을 증진시키는가에 목적 및 중점을 두었습니다. 그러나 공부하는 과정에서 저는 영어성경학교 교재 개발의 주목적은 하나님 말씀을 바르게 전달하는 것이라는 사실을 깨달았습니다. '영어는 단지 하나님의 말씀을 가르치는 도구'라는 분명한 생각을 가지게 된 것이죠.

이 책의 목적은 구약의 인물들을 중심으로
하나님의 말씀을 배우는 것입니다!

이를 배우는 과정에 영어 교육적 방법론을 도입하였습니다. 각 과마다 영어의 네 가지 능력, 듣기(listening), 말하기(speaking), 읽기(reading), 쓰기(writing) 능력을 종합적으로 증진시킬 수 있는 코너를 구성하였습니다.

〈Who Am I?〉 코너는 영어를 들으며 누구에 대해 말하는지 알아보는 장으로, 주로 듣기와 말하기 훈련을 하는 부분입니다. 이 부분에서는 책의 마지막 부분에 마련해둔 영영사전(Index Dictionary)을 활용하여 영어 어휘 공부를 함께 할 수 있도록 하였습니다.

〈Grammar Points〉 코너는 꼭 알아두어야 할 기본 문법들을 알기 쉽게 공부하는 부분입니다.

〈Let's Talk〉 코너는 말하기 훈련을 하는 부분입니다. 앞의 본문에서 나온 문장을 패턴 중심으로 엄선해 살아 있는 실생활 표현을 익히는 것을 목적으로 하였습니다.

〈Confession & Prayer〉 코너는 읽기와 쓰기를 훈련할 수 있는 부분입니다. 이 코너는 특히 하나님의 말씀을 다시 한 번 진중하게 생각해보고 서로의 생각을 나눠보는 부분이기도 합니다. 영어로 기도를 쓰는 훈련을 할 수 있는 코너도 마련해 두었습니다. 영어권 아이들이 쓴 기도문이나 전통적인 좋은 기도문을 소개한 후 이 기도문에 따라 영어로 직접 자신만의 기도문을 써보고 말해보는 훈련도 할 수 있도록 했습니다.

〈A Poem & Song〉은 노래를 통해 하나님의 말씀을 기억하고 영어 능력을 증진시키는 부분입니다. www.sheilahamil.co.uk에 들어가 직접 애니메이션을 보면서 노래를 함께 익힐 수 있다는 점에서 매우 효과적입니다.

이 책의 가장 큰 특징은 교사가 꼭 원어민이어야 할 필요는 없다는 점입니다!

단계별로 구성된 체계적이고 친절한 코너 덕분에 학생별 맞춤형 학습을 이끌 수 있을 뿐만 아니라, 전문 영어 성우가 읽는 오디오와 www.sheilahamil.co.uk에서 보여주는 동영상을 활용하면 원어민이 아니더라도 충분히 이 책을 가르칠 수 있습니다.

이 책은 영어성경 교재를 개발하고자 하는 제 바람의 첫발입니다. 이 첫발을 내딛도록 도와주신 하나님께 깊은 감사를 드립니다. 쉽지 않은 여건에서도 저를 믿어주시고 도와주신 감리회 본부 교육국의 김낙환 총무님과 정현범 목사님께 감사드립니다. 바쁜 일정 중에서도 출판을 서둘러주신 출판국의 한만철 목사님께도 감사드립니다. 그리고 무엇보다도 편집진들에게 감사드립니다. 이들은 모두 국내 유수 영어 전문 출판사의 편집을 하는 이들로 봉사하는 마음으로 이 책을 함께 작업하였습니다. 마지막으로 항상 일에 바쁜 아내와 엄마를 이해하고 사랑으로 기다려주는 가족들에게 감사와 사랑을 보냅니다.

Study God's Precious Word! God's Word Is A Living Word!

Greetings to you all, dear readers, as you study God's precious word. May I recommend this project of Professor Hyunju Lee to you.

Always remember God's word is a living word, which will speak to your heart the more you read it.

In Isaiah 55:11 we learn that the word that goes out from God's mouth, will never return to him empty without accomplishing all that he desires and will achieve the purpose for which it was sent.

It is a word we must revere, respect, and try to memorise so we can draw from it like water from a deep well. Drink from it and drench yourself in it. If a particular verse calls out to you, stay with it, bathe in it before you continue reading.

May God's word open your eyes and fill your hearts with His wisdom, His love and peace.

My love and blessings to you all *Sheila*

* Reverend Sheila Hamil has been working on the project called KALEIDOSCOPE OF CHARACTERS, a collection of 48 'All-Age' songs inspired by stories from the Old Testament, for spreading God's Words all over the world. She lives in England.

Learn English Using Bible Stories!

Hyunju Lee writes an excellent resource to help Korean students learn English using Bible stories. The lessons are entertaining and provide a variety of activities that will help students learn vocabulary and grammar. At the same time, students will learn basic biblical history. The use of a repetitive structure provides familiarity to each lesson so that students can anticipate the next activity. Listening, sentence structure, role play, conversations with partners, and prayer are some of the activities that students will enjoy as they learn and practice English skills.

Rebecca Scheirer

* Rebecca Scheirer, the Doctor of Ministry, is a Program Administrator for the Doctor of Ministry Program at Wesley Theological Seminary in Washington, D.C., USA. Dr. Scheirer enjoys helping students navigate the difficulties of doctoral studies, and lives in Kensington, Maryland, with her husband.

이 책은 구약성서에 등장하는 주요 인물들과 하나님의 이야기를 영어로 들여다보며, 그 옛날 신앙 선조들의 말과 행동을 통해 우리 자신의 신앙을 되돌아볼 수 있도록 구성한 책입니다. 따라서 이 책이 이끄는 대로 차근차근 따라가다 보면 자신의 신앙을 공고히 할 수 있음은 물론, 글로벌 크리스천에 부응하는 영어 커뮤니케이션 능력도 키울 수 있습니다. 각 과는 다음과 같은 코너들로 구성되어 있습니다.

Who Am I?

이번 과에서 다루는 구약성서 속 인물에 대해 배우게 됩니다.

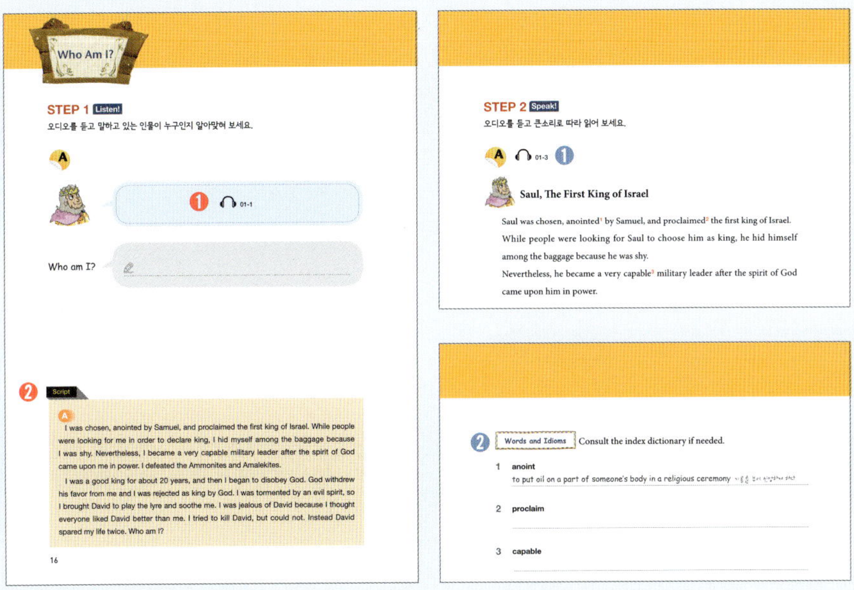
Who Am I?

STEP 1 Listen!
오디오를 듣고 말하고 있는 인물이 누구인지 알아맞혀 보세요.

A

❶ 01-1

Who am I?

❷ Script

A
I was chosen, anointed by Samuel, and proclaimed the first king of Israel. While people were looking for me in order to declare king, I hid myself among the baggage because I was shy. Nevertheless, I became a very capable military leader after the spirit of God came upon me in power. I defeated the Ammonites and Amalekites.

I was a good king for about 20 years, and then I began to disobey God. God withdrew his favor from me and I was rejected as king by God. I was tormented by an evil spirit, so I brought David to play the lyre and soothe me. I was jealous of David because I thought everyone liked David better than me. I tried to kill David, but could not. Instead David spared my life twice. Who am I?

16

STEP 2 Speak!
오디오를 듣고 큰소리로 따라 읽어 보세요.

A 01-3 ❶

Saul, The First King of Israel

Saul was chosen, anointed[1] by Samuel, and proclaimed[2] the first king of Israel.
While people were looking for Saul to choose him as king, he hid himself among the baggage because he was shy.
Nevertheless, he became a very capable[3] military leader after the spirit of God came upon him in power.

❷ Words and Idioms Consult the index dictionary if needed.

1 anoint
to put oil on a part of someone's body in a religious ceremony

2 proclaim

3 capable

STEP 1 Listen!

❶ 성서 속 인물을 바로 알려주기보다는 먼저 오디오로 설명을 들으며, 이번 과에서 알아보게 될 인물이 누구인지를 스스로 생각해보는 시간을 가집니다.

❷ 반드시 오디오를 듣고 인물을 추측해본 다음, 아래 스크립트를 확인하세요.

각 인물에 대한 설명은 각각 두 번씩 들려드립니다.

STEP 2 Speak!

❶ 앞에서 추측해본 인물을 직접 확인해보는 자리입니다. 구약 속 인물에 대한 이야기를 들으며 큰 소리로 여러 번 따라 읽어 보세요.

각 인물에 대한 설명은 두 번씩 녹음되어 있으며, 처음에는 한 문장씩 듣고 따라읽을 수 있게 문장 단위로 pause를 두었습니다.

❷ 〈Words and Idioms〉를 풀어보며 등장한 표현들의 의미를 생각해 보세요. 무슨 의미인지 바로 생각이 안 나면, 책 맨 뒤의 〈Index Dictionary〉를 활용하면 됩니다.

Grammar Points

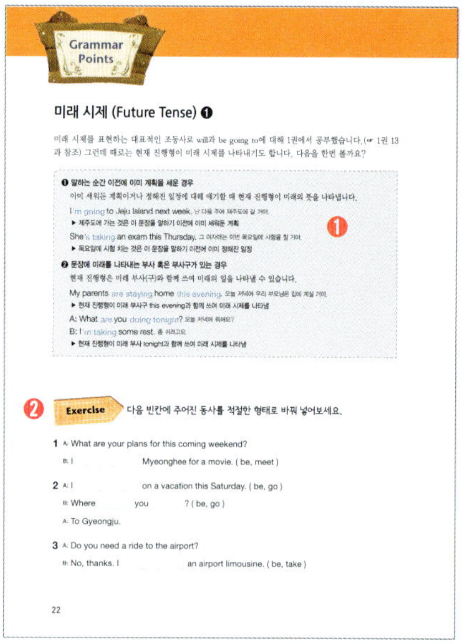
Grammar Points

미래 시제 (Future Tense) ❶

미래 시제를 표현하는 대표적인 조동사로 will과 be going to에 대해 1권에서 공부했습니다.(☞ 1권 13과 참조) 그런데 때로는 현재 진행형이 미래 시제를 나타내기도 합니다. 다음을 한번 볼까요?

❶ 말하는 순간 이전에 이미 계획을 세운 경우
이미 세워둔 계획이거나 정해진 일정에 대해 얘기할 때 현재 진행형이 미래의 뜻을 나타냅니다.
I'm going to Jeju Island next week. 난 다음 주에 제주도에 갈 거야.
▶ 제주도에 가는 것은 이 문장을 말하기 이전에 이미 세워둔 계획
She's taking an exam this Thursday. 그 여자애는 이번 목요일에 시험을 칠 거야.
▶ 목요일에 시험 치는 것은 이 문장을 말하기 이전에 이미 정해진 일정

❷ 문장에 미래를 나타내는 부사 혹은 부사구가 있는 경우
현재 진행형은 미래 부사(구)와 함께 쓰여 미래의 일을 나타낼 수 있습니다.
My parents are staying home this evening. 오늘 저녁에 우리 부모님은 집에 계실 거야.
▶ 현재 진행형이 미래 부사구 this evening과 함께 쓰여 미래 시제를 나타냄
A: What are you doing tonight? 오늘 저녁에 뭐해요?
B: I'm taking some rest. 좀 쉬려고요.
▶ 현재 진행형이 미래 부사 tonight과 함께 쓰여 미래 시제를 나타냄

Exercise 다음 빈칸에 주어진 동사를 적절한 형태로 바꿔 넣어보세요.

1 A: What are your plans for this coming weekend?
B: I ______ Myeonghee for a movie. (be, meet)

2 A: I ______ on a vacation this Saturday. (be, go)
B: Where ______ you ______ ? (be, go)
A: To Gyeongju.

3 A: Do you need a ride to the airport?
B: No, thanks. I ______ an airport limousine. (be, take)

22

영어 성경책을 바르게 읽고 바르게 이해하기 위해서는 기본적인 영어 문법을 알고 있어야 합니다.

❶ 꼭 알아두어야 할 기본 문법을 알기 쉽게 간략히 설명해 두었습니다.

❷ 설명을 차근차근 다 읽고 이해한 다음, Exercise를 통해 실생활에 응용할 수 있는 힘을 기르세요.

Let's Talk

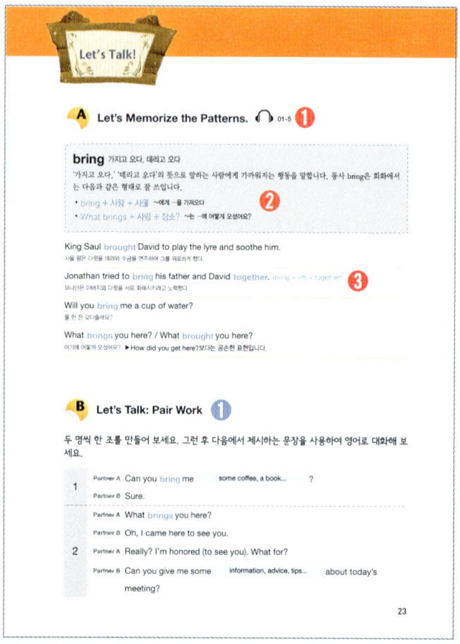
Let's Talk!

A Let's Memorize the Patterns. 01-5

bring 가지고 오다, 데리고 오다
'가지고 오다,' '데리고 오다'의 뜻으로 말하는 사람에게 가까워지는 행동을 말합니다. 동사 bring은 회화에서는 다음과 같은 형태로 잘 쓰입니다.
• bring + 사람 + 사물 ~에게 …을 가져오다
• What brings + 사람 + 장소? ~는 …에 어떻게 오셨어요?

King Saul brought David to play the lyre and soothe him.
사울 왕은 다윗을 데려와 수금을 연주하여 그를 위로하게 했다.

Jonathan tried to bring his father and David together.
요나단은 아버지와 다윗을 서로 화해시키려고 노력했다.

Will you bring me a cup of water?
물 한 잔 갖다줄래요?

What brings you here? / What brought you here?
여기에 어떻게 오셨어요? ▶How did you get here?보다는 공손한 표현입니다.

B Let's Talk: Pair Work

두 명씩 한 조를 만들어 보세요. 그런 후 다음에서 제시하는 문장을 사용하여 영어로 대화해 보세요.

1 Partner A Can you bring me ______ some coffee, a book... ______ ?
Partner B Sure.

2 Partner A What brings you here?
Partner B Oh, I came here to see you.
Partner A Really? I'm honored (to see you). What for?
Partner B Can you give me some ______ information, advice, tips... ______ about today's meeting?

23

영어 성경책을 바르게 읽고 사람들과 신앙을 나누기 위해서는 일상생활에서 흔히 쓰는 표현들을 말할 수 있어야 합니다.

A Let's Memorize the Patterns!

❶ 이야기 속에 등장한 유용한 패턴을 엄선해 말하기 훈련을 해보는 자리입니다.

❷ 먼저 패턴과 의미, 활용법을 숙지하세요.

❸ 그런 다음, 오디오를 듣고 예문을 큰소리로 여러 번 따라 읽어 보세요.

각 문장마다 따라읽을 수 있게 문장길이 만큼 pause가 들어가 있습니다.

B Let's Talk: Pair Work

❶ 바로 앞에서 배운 패턴을 이용해 친구들과 실제 대화 연습을 해보는 자리입니다. 빈칸에 원하는 단어를 넣어 친구와 대화해 보세요.

Confession & Prayer

이번 과에서 배운 인물을 떠올리며 자신의 신앙을 고백하고 기도하는 시간을 가져봅니다.

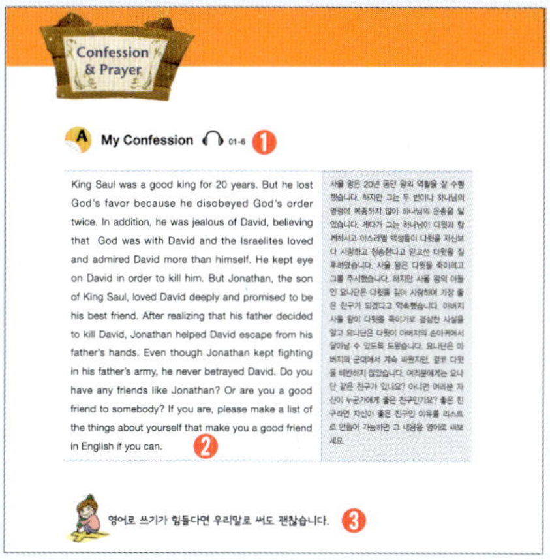
Confession & Prayer

A My Confession 01-6 ①

King Saul was a good king for 20 years. But he lost God's favor because he disobeyed God's order twice. In addition, he was jealous of David, believing that God was with David and the Israelites loved and admired David more than himself. He kept eye on David in order to kill him. But Jonathan, the son of King Saul, loved David deeply and promised to be his best friend. After realizing that his father decided to kill David, Jonathan helped David escape from his father's hands. Even though Jonathan kept fighting in his father's army, he never betrayed David. Do you have any friends like Jonathan? Or are you a good friend to somebody? If you are, please make a list of the things about yourself that make you a good friend in English if you can. ②

영어로 쓰기가 힘들다면 우리말로 써도 괜찮습니다. ③

B Let's Pray! 01-7 ②

Dear God,
Teach me the way of friendship
So that I can be a good friend ①
To someone who needs me,
Or is lonely.
Just as Jonathan befriended David.
Help me be like Jonathan,
A friend to anyone who needs me.

Write a Prayer for Yourself!

Dear God, ③

A My Confession

❶ 성서 속 인물을 통해 하나님이 전하고자 하신 말씀이 무엇인지에 대해 생각하며, 자신의 신앙을 돌아보는 자리입니다.

❷ 영어로 된 글을 차분히 읽으며 이해해 보세요.

🎧 눈을 감고 오디오를 들으며 다시 한 번 글을 이해해 보세요.

❸ 위의 글속에서 던진 질문에 대해 영어 또는 우리말로 자신의 생각을 써보는 자리입니다.

B Let's Pray!

❶ 영어권 기도문을 읽으며 그 의미를 새겨보세요.

❷ 그런 다음 오디오를 듣고, 온 마음을 다해 큰소리로 기도해 보세요.

🎧 기도는 두 번 녹음되어 있으며, 처음에는 한 마디씩 듣고 따라읽을 수 있게 마디 단위로 pause를 두었습니다.

❸ 자신이 하나님께 드리고 싶은 기도를 직접 영어로 적어 보는 자리입니다.

A Poem & Song

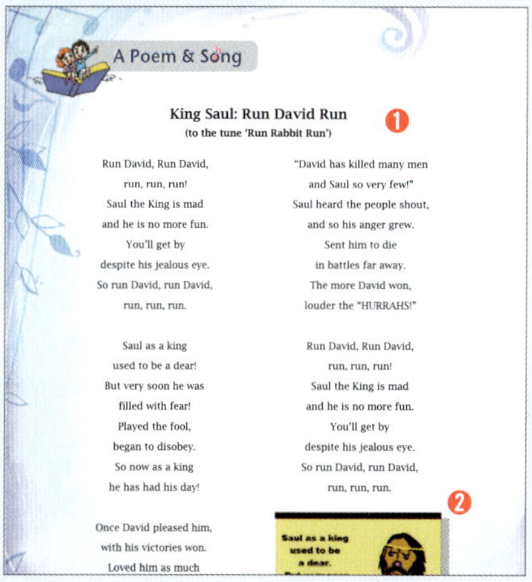
A Poem & Song

King Saul: Run David Run ①
(to the tune 'Run Rabbit Run')

Run David, Run David,
run, run, run!
Saul the King is mad
and he is no more fun.
You'll get by
despite his jealous eye.
So run David, run David,
run, run, run.

Saul as a king
used to be a dear!
But very soon he was
filled with fear!
Played the fool,
began to disobey.
So now as a king
he has had his day!

Once David pleased him,
with his victories won.
Loved him as much

"David has killed many men
and Saul so very few!"
Saul heard the people shout,
and so his anger grew.
Sent him to die
in battles far away.
The more David won,
louder the "HURRAHS!"

Run David, Run David,
run, run, run!
Saul the King is mad
and he is no more fun.
You'll get by
despite his jealous eye.
So run David, run David,
run, run, run.

② Saul as a king used to be a dear.

노래를 통해 하나님의 말씀을 기억하고 영어 실력을 키우는 자리입니다.

❶ 가사를 소리 내어 읽으며 그 의미를 새겨보세요.

❷ 그런 다음, 동영상을 보고 들으며 노래를 큰소리로 따라 해 보세요.

동영상은 www.sheilahamil.co.uk로 접속해 Music 코너 속 kaleidoscope of characters 메뉴를 클릭하면 볼 수 있습니다.

Contents

MP3 파일은 www.kmcedu.or.kr에서 다운로드 받을 수 있습니다.

The Titles of the Bible Books in English

구약의 '창세기'는 영어로 어떻게 쓸까요? 영어 성경을 읽으려면 이처럼 각 책의 영어 명칭을 알아야 합니다. 모든 책의 이름은 대문자로 시작한다는 점에 주의해 다음을 알아두세요!

The Old Testament 구약

Genesis	(Gen.)	창세기	Ecclesiastes	(Eccles.)	전도서
Exodus	(Exod.)	출애굽기	Song of Songs	(Song of Sol.)	아가
Leviticus	(Lev.)	레위기	Isaiah	(Isa.)	이사야
Numbers	(Num.)	민수기	Jeremiah	(Jer.)	예레미야
Deuteronomy	(Deut.)	신명기	Lamentations	(Lam.)	예레미야애가
Joshua	(Josh.)	여호수아	Ezekiel	(Ezek.)	에스겔
Judges	(Judg.)	사사기	Daniel	(Dan.)	다니엘
Ruth	(Ru)	룻기	Hosea	(Hos)	호세아
1 Samuel	(1 Sam.)	사무엘상	Joel	(Jl)	요엘
2 Samuel	(2 Sam.)	사무엘하	Amos	(Am)	아모스
1 Kings	(1 Kgs)	열왕기상	Obadiah	(Obad.)	오바댜
2 Kings	(2 Kgs)	열왕기하	Jonah	(Jon.)	요나
1 Chronicles	(1 Chron.)	역대상	Micah	(Mic.)	미가
2 Chronicles	(2 Chron.)	역대하	Nahum	(Nah.)	나훔
Ezra	(Ezr)	에스라	Habakkuk	(Hab.)	하박국
Nehemiah	(Neh.)	느헤미야	Zephaniah	(Zeph.)	스바냐
Esther	(Est)	에스더	Haggai	(Hag.)	학개
Job	(Jb)	욥기	Zechariah	(Zech.)	스가랴
Psalms	(Ps.)	시편	Malachi	(Mal.)	말라기
Proverbs	(Prov.)	잠언			

The New Testament 신약

Matthew	(Matt.)	마태복음	1 Timothy	(1 Tim.)	디모데전서
Mark	(Mk)	마가복음	2 Timothy	(2 Tim.)	디모데후서
Luke	(Lk)	누가복음	Titus	(Ti)	디도서
John	(Jn)	요한복음	Philemon	(Philem.)	빌레몬서
Acts	(Acts)	사도행전	Hebrews	(Heb.)	히브리서
Romans	(Rom.)	로마서	James	(Jas)	야고보서
1 Corinthians	(1 Cor.)	고린도전서	1 Peter	(1 Pet.)	베드로전서
2 Corinthians	(2 Cor.)	고린도후서	2 Peter	(2 Pet.)	베드로후서
Galatians	(Gal.)	갈라디아서	1 John	(1 Jn)	요한1서
Ephesians	(Eph.)	에베소서	2 John	(2 Jn)	요한2서
Philippians	(Phil.)	빌립보서	3 John	(3 Jn)	요한3서
Colossians	(Col.)	골로새서	Jude	(Jude)	유다서
1 Thessalonians	(1 Thess.)	데살로니가전서	Revelations	(Rev.)	요한계시록
2 Thessalonians	(2 Thess.)	데살로니가후서			

* 괄호 안은 약자

01

The First King of Israel

"About this time tomorrow I will send you a man from the land of Benjamin. Anoint him leader over my people Israel; he will deliver my people from the hand of the Philistines."

(1 Samuel 9:16)

Who Am I?

STEP 1 Listen!

오디오를 듣고 말하고 있는 인물이 누구인지 알아맞혀 보세요.

A

01-1

Who am I?

Script

A

I was chosen, anointed by Samuel, and proclaimed the first king of Israel. While people were looking for me in order to declare king, I hid myself among the baggage because I was shy. Nevertheless, I became a very capable military leader after the spirit of God came upon me in power. I defeated the Ammonites and Amalekites.

I was a good king for about 20 years, and then I began to disobey God. God withdrew his favor from me and I was rejected as king by God. I was tormented by an evil spirit, so I brought David to play the lyre and soothe me. I was jealous of David because I thought everyone liked David better than me. I tried to kill David, but could not. Instead David spared my life twice. Who am I?

B

01-2

Who am I?

Script

B

My father was the first king of Israel. David and I lived together in the palace and we promised to be best friends. My father was jealous of my best friend, David, because he was loved far more than my father. So I always tried to bring my father and David together.

After I found out that my father was really intent on killing my best friend, I helped him to escape. After David ran away from my father, I continued to fight in my father's army. I was always loyal to my father, to my friend and to God all my life. Who am I?

STEP 2 Speak!

오디오를 듣고 큰소리로 따라 읽어 보세요.

A 01-3

Saul, The First King of Israel

Saul was chosen, anointed[1] by Samuel, and proclaimed[2] the first king of Israel. While people were looking for Saul to choose him as king, he hid himself among the baggage because he was shy.
Nevertheless, he became a very capable[3] military leader after the spirit of God came upon him in power.

Saul was a good king for about 20 years, but he disobeyed[4] God's words twice.
So God withdrew[5] his favor from him and rejected[6] him as king.
Saul was tormented[7] by an evil spirit, so he brought David to play the lyre[8] and soothe[9] him.
Saul was jealous of David because he thought everyone liked David better than him.
So he tried to kill David, but instead David spared his life[10] twice.

Words and Idioms Consult the index dictionary if needed.

1 **anoint**
to put oil on a part of someone's body in a religious ceremony 기름을 부어 신성하게 하다

2 **proclaim**

3 **capable**

4 **disobey**

5 **withdraw**

6 **reject**

7 **torment**

8 **lyre**

9 **soothe**

10 **spare someone's life**

B 01-4

Jonathan: The Son of King Saul

Jonathan, the son of King Saul, was a great warrior.[1]
King Saul was jealous of[2] David because David was loved far more than himself.
In this situation, Jonathan tried to bring his father and David together.[3]

Jonathan found out that his father was really intent on[4] killing his best friend, David, so he helped David to escape.[5]
After David ran away from[6] his father, Jonathan continued to fight in his father's army.
Jonathan was always loyal[7] to his father, to his friend and to God all his life.[8]

Words and Idioms Consult the index dictionary if needed.

1 **warrior**
a soldier, especially in the past 용사, 군인

2 **jealous of**

3 **bring ~ together**

4 **intent on**

5 **escape**

6 **run away from**

7 **loyal**

8 **all one's life**

Think about It! Talk about Saul and Jonathan. Who are they?

Grammar Points

미래 시제 (Future Tense) ❶

미래 시제를 표현하는 대표적인 조동사로 will과 be going to에 대해 1권에서 공부했습니다.(☞ 1권 13과 참조) 그런데 때로는 현재 진행형이 미래 시제를 나타내기도 합니다. 다음을 한번 볼까요?

❶ 말하는 순간 이전에 이미 계획을 세운 경우

이미 세워둔 계획이거나 정해진 일정에 대해 얘기할 때 현재 진행형이 미래의 뜻을 나타냅니다.

I'm going to Jeju Island next week. 난 다음 주에 제주도에 갈 거야.

▶ 제주도에 가는 것은 이 문장을 말하기 이전에 이미 세워둔 계획

She's taking an exam this Thursday. 그 여자애는 이번 목요일에 시험을 칠 거야.

▶ 목요일에 시험 치는 것은 이 문장을 말하기 이전에 이미 정해진 일정

❷ 문장에 미래를 나타내는 부사 혹은 부사구가 있는 경우

현재 진행형은 미래 부사(구)와 함께 쓰여 미래의 일을 나타낼 수 있습니다.

My parents are staying home this evening. 오늘 저녁에 우리 부모님은 집에 계실 거야.

▶ 현재 진행형이 미래 부사구 this evening과 함께 쓰여 미래 시제를 나타냄

A: What are you doing tonight? 오늘 저녁에 뭐해요?

B: I'm taking some rest. 좀 쉬려고요.

▶ 현재 진행형이 미래 부사 tonight과 함께 쓰여 미래 시제를 나타냄

Exercise 다음 빈칸에 주어진 동사를 적절한 형태로 바꿔 넣어보세요.

1 A: What are your plans for this coming weekend?

B: I __________ Myeonghee for a movie. (be, meet)

2 A: I __________ on a vacation this Saturday. (be, go)

B: Where ________ you ________ ? (be, go)

A: To Gyeongju.

3 A: Do you need a ride to the airport?

B: No, thanks. I __________ an airport limousine. (be, take)

Let's Talk!

A Let's Memorize the Patterns. 01-5

bring 가지고 오다, 데리고 오다

'가지고 오다,' '데리고 오다'의 뜻으로 말하는 사람에게 가까워지는 행동을 말합니다. 동사 bring은 회화에서는 다음과 같은 형태로 잘 쓰입니다.

- bring + 사람 + 사물 ~에게 …을 가져오다
- What brings + 사람 + 장소? ~는 …에 어떻게 오셨어요?

King Saul **brought** David to play the lyre and soothe him.
사울 왕은 다윗을 데려와 수금을 연주하여 그를 위로하게 했다.

Jonathan tried to **bring** his father and David **together**. (bring + 사람 + together)
요나단은 아버지와 다윗을 서로 화해시키려고 노력했다.

Will you **bring** me a cup of water?
물 한 잔 갖다줄래요?

What **brings** you here? / What **brought** you here?
여기에 어떻게 오셨어요? ▶How did you get here?보다는 공손한 표현입니다.

B Let's Talk: Pair Work

두 명씩 한 조를 만들어 보세요. 그런 후 다음에서 제시하는 문장을 사용하여 영어로 대화해 보세요.

1

Partner A Can you **bring** me (some coffee, a book...)?

Partner B Sure.

2

Partner A What **brings** you here?

Partner B Oh, I came here to see you.

Partner A Really? I'm honored (to see you). What for?

Partner B Can you give me some (information, advice, tips...) about today's meeting?

Confession & Prayer

A My Confession 01-6

King Saul was a good king for 20 years. But he lost God's favor because he disobeyed God's order twice. In addition, he was jealous of David, believing that God was with David and the Israelites loved and admired David more than himself. He kept eye on David in order to kill him. But Jonathan, the son of King Saul, loved David deeply and promised to be his best friend. After realizing that his father decided to kill David, Jonathan helped David escape from his father's hands. Even though Jonathan kept fighting in his father's army, he never betrayed David. Do you have any friends like Jonathan? Or are you a good friend to somebody? If you are, please make a list of the things about yourself that make you a good friend in English if you can.

사울 왕은 20년 동안 왕의 역활을 잘 수행했습니다. 하지만 그는 두 번이나 하나님의 명령에 복종하지 않아 하나님의 은총을 잃었습니다. 게다가 그는 하나님이 다윗과 함께하시고 이스라엘 백성들이 다윗을 자신보다 사랑하고 칭송한다고 믿고선 다윗을 질투하였습니다. 사울 왕은 다윗을 죽이려고 그를 주시했습니다. 하지만 사울 왕의 아들인 요나단은 다윗을 깊이 사랑하여 가장 좋은 친구가 되겠다고 약속했습니다. 아버지 사울 왕이 다윗을 죽이기로 결심한 사실을 알고 요나단은 다윗이 아버지의 손아귀에서 달아날 수 있도록 도왔습니다. 요나단은 아버지의 군대에서 계속 싸웠지만, 결코 다윗을 배반하지 않았습니다. 여러분에게는 요나단 같은 친구가 있나요? 아니면 여러분 자신이 누군가에게 좋은 친구인가요? 좋은 친구라면 자신이 좋은 친구인 이유를 리스트로 만들어 가능하면 그 내용을 영어로 써보세요.

영어로 쓰기가 힘들다면 우리말로 써도 괜찮습니다.

B Let's Pray! 01-7

친구란 정말 소중한 존재이죠. 그러나 가끔 우리는 친구에게 좋은 친구가 되어주기를 바라기만 할 때가 있습니다. 이제부터는 친구한테 여러분이 좋은 친구라는 걸 보여주세요. 오늘은 나부터 먼저 좋은 친구가 될 수 있도록 주님께 기도드려 봐요!

Dear God,
Teach me the way of friendship
So that I can be a good friend
To someone who needs me,
Or is lonely.
Just as Jonathan befriended David.
Help me be like Jonathan,
A friend to anyone who needs me.

사랑의 주님,
친구가 되는 방법을 가르쳐 주세요.
제가 좋은 친구가 될 수 있게요.
저를 필요로 하는 누군가에게,
혹은 외로운 누군가에게.
요나단이 다윗에게 친구가 되어주었던 것처럼.
저를 요나단처럼 되게 도와주세요.
저를 필요로 하는 누군가에게 (요나단 같은) 친구가 되게 해주세요.

Write a Prayer for Yourself!

이제 친구를 위한 기도를 써볼까요? 위의 예처럼 간단하게 영어로 기도를 써보세요.

Dear God,

Amen.

A Poem & Song

King Saul: Run David Run

(to the tune 'Run Rabbit Run')

Run David, Run David,
run, run, run!
Saul the King is mad
and he is no more fun.
You'll get by
despite his jealous eye.
So run David, run David,
run, run, run.

Saul as a king
used to be a dear!
But very soon he was
filled with fear!
Played the fool,
began to disobey.
So now as a king
he has had his day!

Once David pleased him,
with his victories won.
Loved him as much
as Jonathan his son.
Raised him high,
but as the time went by,
Saul turned against him,
and I'll tell you why.

"David has killed many men
and Saul so very few!"
Saul heard the people shout,
and so his anger grew.
Sent him to die
in battles far away.
The more David won,
louder the "HURRAHS!"

Run David, Run David,
run, run, run!
Saul the King is mad
and he is no more fun.
You'll get by
despite his jealous eye.
So run David, run David,
run, run, run.

used with permission www.sheilahamil.co.uk

02

The Man after God's Own Heart

The LORD has sought out a man after his own heart and appointed him leader of his people. (1 Samuel 13:14)

Who Am I?

STEP 1 Listen!

오디오를 듣고 말하고 있는 인물이 누구인지 알아맞혀 보세요.

A

02-1

Who am I?

Script

A

I, the youngest of Jesse's sons, was a shepherd. When I was young, I was anointed by Samuel. I became famous as a young brave soldier after I killed the Philistine giant with a sling and a stone.

After King Saul was dead, I became the anointed king of all Israel. I united the kingdom. God gave me the covenant that the throne of my kingdom would be forever through Nathan, the prophet.

I loved to worship God with songs. I wrote many songs myself and those songs were included in Psalms. I reigned for forty years. Who am I?

B

02-2

Who am I?

Script

B

I was from Philistine. I was nine feet tall! For forty days, I waved my spear and shouted to the Israelites to fight me, but no one would fight me. All the Israelites were scared of me.

One day, the boy came to fight me. He did not wear armor and did not even carry any weapons. The boy shouted to me, “God will give you over to me today!” I did not believe his words. I thought that to kill him would be just a piece of cake. But it was true that God was always on the boy’s side. I fell down to the ground when he threw the stone at me from a sling. I was killed by that boy. Who am I?

STEP 2 Speak!

오디오를 듣고 큰소리로 따라 읽어 보세요.

A 02-3

David: The Man after God's Own Heart

David, the youngest of Jesse's sons, was a shepherd.[1]
When he was young, he was anointed by Samuel.
David became famous as a young brave[2] soldier after he killed the Philistine giant with a sling[3] and a stone.

After King Saul died, David became the anointed king of all Israel.
He united[4] the kingdom.
God gave him the covenant[5] that the throne[6] of his kingdom would be forever[7] through Nathan, the prophet.

David loved to worship[8] God with songs.
He wrote many songs himself and those songs were included[9] in Psalms.
He reigned[10] for forty years.

Words and Idioms Consult the index dictionary if needed.

1 **shepherd**

a man whose job is to take care of sheep 양치기

2 **brave**

3 **sling**

4 **unite**

5 **covenant**

6 **throne**

7 **forever**

8 **worship**

9 **include**

10 **reign**

B 02-4

Goliath: the Philistine Giant

Goliath, the Philistine,[1] was nine feet tall!

For forty days, he waved[2] his spear and shouted to the Israelites to fight him, but no one would fight him.

All the Israelites were scared[3] of him.

One day, the boy who was called David came to fight him.

He did not wear armor[4] and did not even carry any weapons.[5]

David shouted to Goliath, "God will give you over to[6] me today!"

Goliath did not believe his words.

He thought that to kill David would be just a piece of cake.[7]

But it was true that God was always on David's side.[8]

Goliath fell down to the ground when David flew the stone to him from a sling.

He was killed by David.

Words and Idioms Consult the index dictionary if needed.

1 **Philistine**
a member of a race of people who lived in Palestine 블레셋 사람

2 **wave**

3 **scared**

4 **armor**

5 **weapon**

6 **give ~ over to someone**

7 **a piece of cake**

8 **on someone's side**

Think about It! Talk about David and Goliath. Who are they?

Grammar Points

미래 시제 (Future Tense) ❷

시간을 지시하는 접속사 before, after, when, as soon as, until이 이끄는 절에서는 현재 시제가 미래를 대신합니다.

Before I go to school, I'm going to eat breakfast. 학교 가기 전에 아침밥을 먹을 거야.

▶ 밥 먹은 후 학교에 가는 것이므로 미래 시제이지만 before라는 접속사 때문에 현재 시제를 씀

After I eat breakfast, I'm going to school. 난 아침밥 먹고 나서 학교에 갈 거야.

▶ 아직 밥을 먹지 않아 미래의 일을 말하지만 after 접속사 때문에 현재 시제를 씀

주의! 위 문장들에서 보는 바와 같이 접속사가 이끄는 절이 맨 앞에 나올 때는 절이 끝나는 곳에 콤마를 씁니다. 하지만 절이 이끄는 문장이 뒤에 올 때는 앞에 콤마가 없습니다.

I'm going to eat breakfast before I go to school.

I'm going to school after I eat breakfast.

Exercise 다음 빈칸에 주어진 동사를 적절한 형태로 바꿔 넣어보세요.

1 It's snowing outside. As soon as the snow ________, I'm going to the bookstore. (stop)

2 I'll give Jinsu your message when I ________ her. (see)

3 Before I ________ to the academy, I'm going to stop at MacDonald's. (go)

4 I'll stay home until you ________ me. (call)

5 After I ________ a shower, I'll go to bed. (take)

Let's Talk!

A Let's Memorize the Patterns. 02-5

a piece of cake 식은 죽 먹기

우리말로 아주 쉬운 것을 '식은 죽 먹기'라고 말합니다. 영어에도 이와 같은 표현이 있습니다. 바로 a piece of cake이죠. 이밖에도 '아주 쉽다'와 반대로 '아주 어렵다'는 의미로 곧잘 쓰이는 표현들을 아래에 정리해 두었습니다. 네이티브의 음성을 듣고 따라읽으며 입에 배게 익혀두세요.

It's **a piece of cake**. 식은 죽 먹기예요.

A: How was the math exam? 수학 시험 어땠어?
B: It was **a piece of cake**. 식은 죽 먹기였어.

It was **nothing**. 별거 아녔어. (너무 쉬웠어.)

The math exam was **no problem**. 수학 시험 너무 쉬웠어.

It was **a breeze**. 완전 껌이었어.
▶산들바람(breeze)이 살랑살랑 부는 것처럼 쉽다는 이야기인 거죠.

It was **hard/difficult**. 어려웠어.

It was a **very tough** exam. 너무 어려운 시험이었어.

B Let's Talk: Pair Work

두 명씩 한 조를 만들어 보세요. 그런 후 다음에 제시된 문장을 사용하여 시험이 어땠는지 서로 묻고, 쉬웠다거나 어려웠다는 대답을 해보세요.

1
Partner A How was ________ ?
Partner B It was ________ .

과목 종류 국어 **Korean** | 한문 **Chinese writing** | 중국어 **Chinese** | 일본어 **Japanese** | 영어 **English** | 과학 **science** | 생물 **biology** | 화학 **chemistry** | 지리 **geography** | 역사 **history** | 윤리 **ethics** | 사회 **social studies** | 미술 **art** | 가정 **home economics** | 수학 **math(ematics)** | 체육 **PE (physical education)**
▶ 이런 과목명 뒤에 exam을 붙여 활용해 보세요. 그 과목 시험을 의미합니다.

시험 종류 중간고사 **mid-term exam** | 학기말 고사 **final exam** | 쪽지 시험 **quiz**

Confession & Prayer

A My Confession 02-6

David believed that God was always on his side. This sincere belief made David a brave man. When he was a boy, he usually took care of sheep for his father. He was not scared of lions and bears because he believed that God always protected him and his sheep from the attacks of wild animals. Whenever a lion or a bear came and took a lamb from the flock, he went after it, knocked it down and rescued the lamb. He could also stand alone in front of Goliath without any armor or weapons because he believed that God would give him the power to defeat him. Do you believe God is always on your side like David? Do you have anything to be afraid of? Write some of the things that you are afraid of. Then write your prayers to God for giving you the courage to be brave like David whenever you are afraid. Please write them in English if you can.

다윗은 하나님이 항상 자신의 편임을 믿었습니다. 이 신실한 믿음 때문에 다윗은 용감한 사람이 되었죠. 어렸을 때 다윗은 아버지를 위해 양을 돌보는 일이 일상이었습니다. 다윗은 하나님이 야생 동물의 공격으로부터 자신과 양들을 보호해 주신다고 믿었기 때문에 사자와 곰을 두려워하지 않았습니다. 사자나 곰이 와서 양떼에서 양을 채갈 때면 다윗은 쫓아가 사자나 곰을 물리치고 양을 구하였죠. 다윗은 또한 갑옷도 입지 않고 무기도 없이 골리앗 앞에 홀로 맞설 수 있었는데, 이는 하나님이 자신에게 골리앗을 물리칠 힘을 줄 것이라 믿었기 때문입니다. 여러분은 다윗처럼 하나님이 항상 자신의 편이라 믿나요? 여러분은 두려워하는 것이 없나요? 여러분이 두려워하는 것들을 써보세요. 그런 후 하나님께 여러분이 두려워질 때마다 다윗처럼 용감해질 용기를 달라고 기도문을 써보세요. 가능하면 그 내용을 영어로 써보세요.

영어로 쓰기가 힘들다면 우리말로 써도 괜찮습니다.

B Let's Memorize David's Song! 02-7

다음은 시편 23편에 기록되어 있는 다윗 왕이 쓴 찬양입니다. 다음의 시를 큰 소리로 따라읽으며 가능하다면 외워보세요.

The Lord is my shepherd, I shall not be in want.
He makes me lie down in green pastures,
he leads me beside quiet waters,
he restores my soul.
He guides me in paths of righteousness
for his name's sake.
Even though I walk
through the valley of the shadow of death,
I will fear no evil,
for you are with me;
your rod and your staff,
they comfort me.
You prepare a table before me
in the presence of my enemies.
You anoint my head with oil;
my cup overflows.
Surely goodness and love will follow me
all the days of my life,
and I will dwell in the house of the LORD
forever.

(Psalms 23)

여호와는 나의 목자시니 내게 부족함이 없으리로다.
그가 나를 푸른 풀밭에 누이시며
쉴 만한 물가로 인도하시는도다.
내 영혼을 소생시키시고,
자기 이름을 위하여
의의 길로 인도하시는도다.
내가 사망의 음침한 골짜기로
다닐지라도
해를 두려워하지 않을 것은
주께서 나와 함께하심이라
주의 지팡이와 막대기가
나를 안위하시나이다.
주께서 내 원수의 목전에서
내게 상을 차려 주시고
기름을 내 머리에 부으셨으니
내 잔이 넘치나이다.
내 평생에
선하심과 인자하심이 반드시 나를 따르리니
내가 여호와의 집에
영원히 살리로다.

(시편 23편)

A Poem & Song

David and Goliath

(to the tune 'Marching through Georgia')

David came with food one day,
to the Valley of Elah,
looking for his brothers
Who were fighting in a war.
And as he neared the battle scene,
saw men afraid to fight,
challenged by the giant Goliath.

When David heard,
he made his mind up there.
"I'll fight him as
with lion and with bear!"
And so they put some armour on him,
but it was no use!
Instead he faced the giant without it.

Taking up his staff,
he chose five pebbles from the stream.
Then with sling and stones in hand
approached the Philistine!
And as he looked upon the lad,
could not believe his eyes!
"He's just a BOY!" hissed Goliath.

"Am I... a dog,
you come to me with sticks?
Come here, my lad,
I'll cut you into bits.
I'll give your flesh up to the birds,
and beasts will eat your bones.
How dare they send such a weakling!"

"Here you come with sword and spear,
and javelin as well!
But I'm here in the name of God,
The Lord of Israel,"
said David, "I will strike you down,
and I'll cut off your head!
The world will know
the Lord God of Israel!"

"For we are saved,
by neither spear or sword.
We're saved because
the battle is the Lord's!
Your army will be food for birds,
and beasts will eat your bones.
Mighty is the Lord God of Israel!"

Goliath moved in closer now,
his face an angry red.
David slung his little stone,
which struck him on the head.
Then David took the giant's sword,
made sure that he was dead.
Now who's afraid of Goliath?

"Hurray! Hurrah!
Who is this brave young man?"
said Saul the King,
"go find out if you can!"
They brought before him Jesse's son,
the lad from Bethlehem.
Everyone knew God was with him!

used with permission www.sheilahamil.co.uk

03

The King of Great Wisdom

God gave Solomon wisdom and very great insight, and a breadth of understanding as measureless as the sand on the seashore. (1 Kings 4:29)

Who Am I?

STEP 1 Listen!

오디오를 듣고 말하고 있는 인물이 누구인지 알아맞혀 보세요.

A

03-1

Who am I? ______________________

Script

A

I was the third king of Israel. When I became a king, God asked me in a dream, "What would you like me to give you?" I answered, "Could you give me wisdom so that I will know the difference between right and wrong?" God was pleased with my answer, so He gave me riches and honor as well as wisdom.

I was famous as the wisest king. People from all over the world came to see me. Even the queen of Sheba came from far away to ask me questions.

I built the Temple and dedicated it to God. God was happy with the temple and all the people of Israel were also happy to have a new place to worship. I built my palace as well. I reigned for forty years. Who am I?

B

03-2

Who am I?

Script

B

When I woke up, I was surprised to see that my baby was dead. My baby was fine last night, so I checked him carefully. As a result, I found out that the dead boy was not mine, but the baby of the woman living in the same house. I asked her to give back my baby, but she refused. She even insisted that the living baby was hers, so we went to King Solomon to judge this case.

After he listened to our words, he ordered his men to cut my baby in two and give half to each one of us. I was really scared that my baby would be killed, so I answered that the baby was not mine. Surprisingly, King Solomon ordered them to give that baby to me. How wise our king was! Who am I?

STEP 2 Speak!

오디오를 듣고 큰소리로 따라 읽어 보세요.

A 03-3

Solomon: King of Great Wisdom

Solomon was the third[1] king of Israel.

When he became a king, God asked[2] him in a dream, "What would you like me to give you?"

Solomon answered, "Could you give me wisdom[3] so that I will know the difference[4] between right and wrong?"

God was pleased with his answer, so He gave him riches[5] and honor as well as[6] wisdom.

He was famous as the wisest[7] king.

People from all over the world came to see him.

Even the queen of Sheba came from far away to ask him questions.

Solomon built the Temple and dedicated[8] it to God.

God was happy with the temple and all the people of Israel were also happy to have a new place to worship.

He built his palace as well.[9]

He reigned[10] for forty years.

Words and Idioms Consult the index dictionary if needed.

1 **third**
in the place or position counted as number 3 세 번째의

2 **ask**

3 **wisdom**

4 **difference**

5 **riches** *(n.)*

6 **as well as something/somebody**

7 **wise**

8 **dedicate**

9 **as well**

10 **reign**

B 03-4

True Mother of the Baby

When the mother woke up,[1] she was very surprised to see that her baby was dead.

After checking[2] her baby carefully, she found out that the dead boy was not hers, but[3] the baby of the woman living in the same house.

The mother asked her to[4] give back[5] her baby, but she insisted[6] that he was her baby.

So the two mothers went to King Solomon to find out who the true mother was.

After listening to their words, King Solomon ordered[7] his men to cut[8] the living baby in two and give half to each woman.

The true mother was very scared that her living baby would be killed, so she answered that the baby was not her own.

Surprisingly, King Solomon ordered them to give that baby to the true mother.

How wise King Solomon was!

Words and Idioms Consult the index dictionary if needed.

1 **wake up**

to stop sleeping 잠에서 깨다, 일어나다

2 **check**

3 **not A(,) but B**

4 **ask someone to do**

5 **give back**

6 **insist**

7 **order**

8 **cut**

Think about It! Talk about Solomon. Who is he?

Grammar Points

진행 시제를 쓰지 못하는 상태 동사 (non-action verbs)

동사들 중에는 진행형을 쓰지 못하는 것들이 있습니다. 이를 상태 동사(non-action verbs)라 부르죠.

❶ 상태 동사의 종류

진행형을 쓰지 못하는 상태 동사에는 다음과 같은 것들이 있습니다.

hear	see	sound	believe	know	think	understand
be	seem	have	possess	want	like	love
hate	forget	remember				

❷ 뜻이 달라지면 진행형을 쓰기도 하는 have와 think

위에서 언급한 동사들 중에서 have와 think처럼 진행형을 쓰는 경우가 있습니다. 하지만 이와 같은 경우에는 뜻이 달라지죠.

Miyeong **has** a new Tablet PC. 미영이는 신상 태블릿 피시를 가지고 있다.

▶ have가 '소유하다'의 의미인 경우 진행형으로 쓸 수 없음

I'**m having** a good time. 나는 좋은 시간을 보내고 있어.

▶ have는 '소유하다'의 의미가 아니라 '보내다'의 의미. have a bad time(안 좋은 시간을 보내다), have trouble(어려움을 겪다), have a problem(문제가 있다) 등의 표현으로 쓰일 경우 진행형 가능

Jeongmin **is having** breakfast. 정민이는 아침을 먹고 있어.

▶ have는 '먹다'의 의미. have a snack(간식을 먹다), have lunch/dinner(점심/저녁을 먹다)도 이와 같은 경우

I **think** the Bible is great. 난 성경이 대단하다고 생각한다.

▶ think가 이와 같이 '믿다'의 의미인 경우 진행형을 쓰지 못함

A: What **are** you **thinking**? 무엇을 생각하고 있니?
B: I'**m thinking about** today's worship. 오늘 예배에 대해 생각하고 있어.

▶ 마음속에 진행되고 있는 생각을 묻거나 답할 때는 진행형

Exercise 주어진 동사를 현재 시제와 현재 진행 시제 중 적절한 형태로 넣어보세요.

1 Mom ______ exercise is good for me. (think)

2 I ______ a good friend. His name is Minsu. (have)

3 She ______ about going to Duksu Palace. (think)

4 A: ______ you ______ some help? (need) B: Yes, thank you.

Let's Talk!

A Let's Memorize the Patterns. 03-5

want to vs. would like to ~하고 싶다

둘 다 우리말로는 모두 '~하고 싶다'란 의미로, to 뒤에는 동사원형을 쓰죠. 하지만 would like to가 want to 보다 부드럽고 공손한 어감을 주는 말입니다.

I **want to** buy a history book. 역사책을 사고 싶은데요.

I'**d like to** buy a history book. 역사책을 사고 싶습니다.

What **would** you **like** me **to** give you? 내게 무엇을 받기를 원하느냐?

▶ 하나님께서 솔로몬에게 이렇게 부드럽고 공손한 표현을 사용해서 질문하셨습니다. 그러자 솔로몬도 Could를 사용하여 매우 정중하게 답하죠.

Could you give me wisdom so that I will know the difference between right and wrong?

제게 지혜를 주십시오. 그래서 옳고 그른 것의 차이를 알게 해주십시오.

▶ 위의 질문에 대한 솔로몬의 정중한 대답입니다. 여기서 〈Could you + 동사원형 ~?〉의 패턴도 기억해 두세요. 이와 같은 정중한 표현은 많이 쓰면 쓸수록 좋습니다.

B Let's Talk: Pair Work

두 명씩 한 조를 만들어 보세요. 그런 후 다음의 문장을 활용해 주어진 대화를 번갈아 말해보세요.

얘기 좀 하자고 할 때	물어볼 게 있다고 할 때
I **want to** talk with you. I'**d like to** have a talk with you. I **would like to** have a word with you. (좀 심각한 상황일 때 이렇게 말함)	I **want to** ask you something. I **would like to** ask you a question.

1

Partner A I ______________ .

Partner B Sure. What is it?

or Sure. **Could you** tell me what it is?

Confession & Prayer

A My Confession 03-6

King Solomon intended to build a temple for the Name of the LORD. He planned to build the best and most beautiful temple in the world. He asked his people to find the best trees of all. He also ordered them to cut big stones for the walls. He decorated God's temple with gold and the best cloths. When the temple was finished after seven years of work, King Solomon had a celebration for dedicating the temple to God. God was very pleased with his temple. God promised that if Solomon would walk with God with integrity of heart and uprightness, and follow His commandments, a successor to his throne would not fail. (1 Kings 9:4-5) Please read God's promises to King Solomon again. After that, think about what is the most important thing in order to be a true Christian? Share your idea with group members and write down your idea in English if possible.

솔로몬은 주님의 이름을 위하여 성전을 짓기로 했습니다. 세상에서 가장 좋고 아름다운 성전을 지으려고 계획했죠. 솔로몬은 백성들에게 세상에서 제일 좋은 나무를 찾으라고 명했습니다. 또 큰 돌을 잘라 성전의 벽을 만들도록 했죠. 하나님의 성전을 금과 최고의 천으로 장식했습니다. 7년간의 공사 끝에 성전이 완성되자 솔로몬 왕은 하나님께 성전을 봉헌하는 봉헌식을 했습니다. 하나님은 매우 기뻐하셨습니다. 하나님은 만일 솔로몬이 마음을 온전히 하고 바르게 하여 하나님과 함께하며 하나님의 명령에 따른다면 그의 왕위를 영원히 견고하게 하리라 약속하셨습니다. (열왕기상 9:4-5) 이제 하나님께서 솔로몬에게 한 약속들을 다시 읽어보세요. 그런 후 진정한 그리스도인이 되기 위해 가장 중요한 것이 무엇인지 생각해 보세요. 다른 친구들과 이야기를 나누어 본 후 여러분의 생각을 가능하면 영어로 써보세요.

영어로 쓰기가 힘들다면 우리말로 써도 괜찮습니다.

B Let's Memorize Solomon's Proverbs! 03-7

다음은 현명한 말에 대한 솔로몬의 잠언을 바탕으로 한 기도문입니다. 다음을 큰 소리로 따라읽으며 외워보세요.

Speak Wisely

Good people must be wise
in what they say,
They should speak gently
to avoid quarrels;
they should be kind and encouraging,
not cruel and insulting,
they should never whisper untrue things about others,
but always tell the truth.

(Proverbs 15:1, 4 & 16:27-28)

현명하게 말하기

의인은 말을 함에 있어
현명해야만 합니다.
의인은 온화하게 말하여
다툼을 피해야 합니다.
의인은 친절하고 용기를 북돋아주며,
잔인하거나 모욕적인 말을 하지 않아야
합니다.
의인은 다른 사람에 대해 절대 거짓을
속삭이지 말아야 하며,
항상 진실만을 말해야 합니다.

(잠언 15:1, 4 & 16:27-28)

Write a Prayer for Yourself!

현명하게 말할 수 있는 지혜를 구하는 마음으로 위의 기도문을 직접 써보세요.

A Poem & Song

King Solomon's Judgement

(to the tune 'Ten Green Bottles')

Two angry women came before the king;
both were unhappy, both were arguing.
Both had had babies, but one of them had died.
So who was the mother of the living child?

One said, "This baby is definitely mine,
but she lay upon hers sometime in the night!
She stole my baby, took him to her bed;
and left hers beside me, I woke to find him dead!"

The other woman cursed her, said that she had lied.
"My son's the live one, yours the one that died!"
"That's not true!" said the first one angrily.
"Yours is the dead one, now give my son to me!"

Solomon had heard enough and called out for a sword,
for he had a plan to decide who was the fraud.
Gave a command to cut the child in two!
"Give half to each woman, wouldn't that be good?"

"STOP, DON'T KILL HIM! Let her have the child!"
said one, but the other was happy to comply.
And so King Solomon, made it very clear,
which one was the mother, and which one was the liar!

used with permission www.sheilahamil.co.uk

04

Two Kings Who Repaired God's House

Joash did what was right in the eyes of the LORD all the years Jehoiada the priest instructed him. (2 Kings 12:2)

Who Am I?

STEP 1 Listen!

오디오를 듣고 말하고 있는 인물이 누구인지 알아맞혀 보세요.

A

04-1

Who am I?

Script

A

I was born as the son of Ahaziah, king of Judah. I was a prince, but my father was killed by Jehu, king of Israel. After realizing that my father was dead, my grandmother tried to kill all my royal family. Jehosheba, my father's sister, stole me from among royal princes and hid my nurse and me in a bedroom.

When I was seven years old, some soldiers came and showed me to all the people. And the people cheered for me to be their new king because I was the only direct descendant of King David's royal family.

After I became a king, I found that the temple of the LORD had been damaged a lot. So I put a big box by the temple and let the people put their money into that box. I had the money to fix the temple, so I repaired it and everybody was happy with the temple. I reigned over my kingdom for forty years. Who am I?

B

04-2

Who am I?

Script

B

I became a king of Judah when I was eight years old. I was known as the faithful king. My father worshipped idols, but I loved the LORD God and sought to please him in every way. So I destroyed the idols in Judah and sent workers to repair the temple of the LORD.

While the workers were cleaning the temple, they found Israel's treasure, the Book of the Law written by Moses. The law warned Israel that if they disobeyed the ten commandments, God would send great trouble upon them. So I asked God for forgiveness for the sins of my people. I brought the people back to the worship and laws of God. I reigned for thirty-one years. Who am I?

STEP 2 Speak!

오디오를 듣고 큰소리로 따라 읽어 보세요.

A 04-3

Joash: A Boy King

Joash was born as the son of Ahaziah, king of Judah.

He was a prince, but his father was killed by Jehu, king of Israel.

After realizing that the king was dead, Athaliah, Joash's grandmother, tried to kill all his royal[1] family.

Jehosheba, the king's sister, stole[2] Joash from among royal princes and hid[3] him and his nurse[4] in a bedroom.

When Joash was seven years old, some soldiers came to him and showed him to all the people.

And the people cheered[5] for Joash to be their new king because he was the only direct descendant[6] of King David's royal family.

After Joash became a king, he found that the temple of the LORD had been damaged[7] a lot.

So he put a big box by the temple and let the people put their money into[8] that box.

When Joash had the money to fix[9] the temple, he repaired[10] it and everybody was happy with the temple.

King Joash reigned over his kingdom for forty years.

Words and Idioms Consult the index dictionary if needed.

1 **royal**

relating to a king or queen or the members of their family 왕가의, 왕족의

2 **steal**

3 **hide**

4 **nurse**

5 **cheer**

6 **descendant**

7 **damage**

8 **put A into B**

9 **fix**

10 **repair**

B 04-4

Josiah: The King Who Found Israel's Treasure

Josiah became king of Judah when he was eight years old.

He was known as the faithful[1] king.

His father, King Amon, worshipped idols,[2] but Josiah loved the LORD God and sought to[3] please Him in every way.

So Josiah destroyed the idols in Judah and sent workers to repair the temple of the LORD.

While the workers were cleaning the temple, they found Israel's treasure,[4] the Book of the Law written by Moses.

The law warned[5] Israel that if they disobeyed the ten commandments,[6] God would send great trouble upon them.

Josiah asked God for forgiveness[7] for the sins[8] of his people.

He brought the people back to the worship and laws of God.

He reigned for thirty-one years.

Words and Idioms Consult the index dictionary if needed.

1 **faithful**
continuing to do or believe something, even in a difficult situation 신실한

2 **idol**

3 **seek to do**

4 **treasure**

5 **warn**

6 **commandment**

7 **ask someone for forgiveness**

8 **sin**

Think about It! Talk about Joash and Josiah. Who are they?

Grammar Points

현재완료 시제 (Present Perfect Tense) ❶

현재완료 시제(have + p.p.)는 우리말에는 없기 때문에 단번에 친숙해지기는 힘듭니다. 하지만 현재완료 시제의 개념을 잘 이해한 다음, 예문을 통해 자꾸 접하다보면 어느새 당연한 듯 쓰게 될 것입니다.

❶ 현재완료 시제의 개념

아래 그림처럼 과거의 어느 한 순간부터 현재 말하는 순간까지 어떤 일을 계속하거나 끝냈다는 것을 나타내는 것이 현재완료 시제입니다. 이 현재완료 시제는 경험, 계속, 완료, 결과의 4가지 용법이 있습니다.

❷ 경험을 나타내는 현재완료: have/has + p.p. ~해 본 적이 있다

현재완료의 4가지 용법 중 이번 과에서는 먼저 우리가 가장 많이 쓰는 경험적 용법에 대해 살펴보죠.

I have been to Jerusalem. 난 예루살렘에 가본 적이 있다.

I have read *Harry Potter*. 난 〈해리포터〉를 읽은 적이 있다.

▶ 참고로 책 이름은 이탤릭체 또는 따옴표로 표기합니다.

Have you eaten sushi? 초밥을 먹어본 적이 있나요?

Exercise 다음 우리말을 영어로 써보세요.

1 우리 가족(My family)은 경주(Gyeongju)에 가본 적이 있다.

2 그 영화를 본 적이 있나요?

3 난 이전에(before) 그를 만난 적이 있다.

Let's Talk!

A Let's Memorize the Patterns. 04-5

find ~을 발견하다, 찾다 **vs. find out** ~을 발견하다, 알게 되다

find와 find out은 우리말로 모두 '~을 발견하다'입니다. 하지만 이 두 단어는 뉘앙스의 차이가 약간 있습니다. find는 우리가 알고 있는 넓은 의미로 '발견하다'입니다. 이와 달리 find out은 연구를 하거나 경험을 해서 어떤 사실, 정보, 지식들을 알게 된 경우를 말합니다. find out은 영어에서 많이 사용되는 표현이니 기억해 주세요.

I'm sure you'll **find** a way. 길을 찾으실 수 있을 거예요.

▶ 길을 찾는다고 하거나, 백화점 등에서 매장이 있는 곳을 물을 경우 동사 find를 이용하면 좋습니다.

It's kind of you to visit me in the hospital, but how did you **find out** about my illness?

면회 와줘서 고마워요. 그런데 제가 아픈 건 어떻게 아셨어요?

▶ 어떤 사실을 어떻게 알았냐고 물을 때는 find out을 이용하면 됩니다.

B Let's Talk: Pair Work

두 명씩 한 조를 만들어 보세요. 그런 후 다음 대화를 번갈아가며 나눠보세요.

1

Partner A Where can I **find** a grocery store?

Partner B It's on the 3rd floor.

2

Partner A Today is Teacher's Day. There are no classes in the afternoon.

Partner B How did you **find out**?

Partner A It was announced yesterday.

3

Partner A Where can I **find** ______________?

Partner B It's ______________.

쇼핑할 때 위치를 물어볼 만한 장소(가게나 매장 등)

가전제품 home appliances | 문구점 stationery (shop) | 제과점 bakery | 수퍼마켓 supermarket | 사진관 photo shop | 서점 bookstore | 스포츠용품점 sports shop | 상설 할인 매장 discount store | 탈의실 dressing room

Confession & Prayer

A My Confession 04-6

King Joash and King Josiah became kings when they were boys. Both of them were faithful kings. They tried to destroy the idols and let their people obey God's words again. After finding out that God's House had been damaged a lot, they decided to fix it up. But it was not easy for them. King Joash had difficulties collecting enough money to repair it. King Josiah might have had difficulties getting his people's agreement because they had not worshiped in the temple for many years. After overcoming many difficulties, King Joash and King Josiah fixed the temple and let their people worship there again. Considering these two stories, it is very important for us to respect and take care of our church. Think about how you can help in your church. Share your idea with group members and write down your idea in English if possible.

요아스 왕과 요시야 왕은 모두 어렸을 때 왕이 되었습니다. 이들 두 왕은 신실한 왕이었죠. 이들은 모두 우상을 타파하고 백성들로 하여금 다시금 하나님의 말씀에 복종하도록 노력했습니다. 성전이 많이 훼손된 것을 발견하자, 이 두 왕은 성전을 고치기로 결심했습니다. 그러나 이것은 쉬운 일이 아니었죠. 요아스 왕은 성전을 고치는 데 필요한 돈을 모으는 데 어려움을 겪었습니다. 요시야 왕의 경우 오랫동안 백성들이 성전에서 예배를 보지 않았기 때문에 이들의 동의를 얻는 데 어려움을 겪었을지도 모르죠. 수많은 어려움을 극복한 후, 요아스 왕과 요시야 왕은 성전을 수리하고 백성들로 하여금 그곳에서 다시 예배드리도록 했습니다. 이 두 이야기를 볼 때, 교회를 섬기고 돌보는 것은 매우 중요합니다. 이를 위해 교회에서 내가 도울 수 있는 일을 생각해 보세요. 다른 친구들과 이야기를 나누어 본 후 여러분의 생각을 가능하면 영어로 써보세요.

영어로 쓰기가 힘들다면 우리말로 써도 괜찮습니다.

B Let's Remind Ourselves about Moses' Ten Commandments! 04-7

요시야 왕은 모세의 율법서를 발견한 후 백성들에게 모세의 십계명을 지키도록 했습니다. 1권에서 우리가 공부한 모세의 십계명을 다시 한 번 새겨볼까요?

1. You shall have no other gods but Me.
2. Do not treat anything else as God.
3. You shall not use the name of the Lord to swear or curse.
4. You shall keep the Sabbath Day holy.
5. Honour your father and your mother.
6. You shall not commit murder.
7. You shall not commit adultery.
8. You shall not steal.
9. You shall not lie.
10. Do not long for other people's things.

(Exod. 20:3-17)

1. 너는 나 외에는 다른 신들을 네게 두지 말라.
2. 다른 어떤 것도 신으로 섬기지 말라.
3. 너는 여호와의 이름을 망령되게 부르지 말라.
4. 안식일을 거룩하게 지키라.
5. 네 부모를 공경하라.
6. 살인하지 말라.
7. 간음하지 말라.
8. 도둑질하지 말라.
9. 거짓말하지 말라.
10. 네 이웃의 것을 탐내지 말라.

(출애굽기 20:3-17)

Write the Ten Commandments for Yourself!

십계명을 다 기억하고 있나요? 그럼 다음 빈칸에 십계명을 직접 써보세요.

1.

2.

3.

4.

5.

6.

7.

8.

9.

10.

A Poem & Song

If My People

(to the tune 'I Come from Alabama')

When the heavens do not open
and there is no more rain.
When locust hordes devour the land,
whenever there's a plague,
whenever there's a plague,
the Lord says:

"If my people,
all those called by my name,
will pray in all humility,
repent and seek my face,
repent and seek my face;
then I will hear them,
from heaven where I stand.
And I'll forgive their wickedness,
and I will heal their land,
and I will heal their land."

"My eyes they will be opened,
my ears will hear their prayers.
My temple is a holy place,
my eyes and heart are there!
My eyes and heart are there!"

"If my people,
all those called by my name,
will pray in all humility,
repent and seek my face,
repent and seek my face;
then I will hear them,
from heaven where I stand.
And I'll forgive their wickedness,
and I will heal their land,
and I will heal their land,
and I will heal their land."

used with permission www.sheilahamil.co.uk

05

The Man Who Was Fed by Ravens

Then the woman said to Elijah, "Now I know that you are a man of God and that the word of the LORD from your mouth is the truth." (1 Kings 17:24)

Who Am I?

STEP 1 Listen!

오디오를 듣고 말하고 있는 인물이 누구인지 알아맞혀 보세요.

A

05-1

Who am I?

Script

A

My name means "Yahweh is my God." When I was a prophet, King Ahab reigned over Israel. He worshiped idols, so God was angry at him. I was sent to him to deliver God's message. "There will be no rain or dew in Israel until I say so." King Ahab wanted to kill me because of this bad news. God told me to hide from that angry king. While I stayed in a hiding place, God sent ravens to bring bread and meat to me. I drank water from the stream. After three years of hiding, God ordered me to go to King Ahab and give rain to dry lands.

God sent me to the widow who had little food to eat. I multiplied her food according to God's order, and she treated me well with that food. I also revived her son.

I hit the Jordan River with my coat, and it parted. When I walked with Elisha, a chariot of fire took me into the heaven. Who am I?

B

05-2

Who am I?

Script

B

I was queen of Israel and wife of King Ahab. I was notorious as the queen who adored and worshiped my god, Baal.

The lands of Israel became dry after one old man came and delivered bad news that it would not rain for a long time. I believed that my god would answer first when the old man came back and asked us to choose the true God who answered by fire. To my surprise, my god did not answer when the 450 priests called on our god all day. They even cut themselves with swords, but there was no answer. Contrary to my expectation, the old man's god started a fire even though the altar was wet with water. After witnessing this, my people bowed down and worshiped that God as their one true God. Immediately it rained again. I was so furious that I sent him a message that he would die like my priests. But I could not kill him because he ran away and was led by his God. Who am I?

STEP 2 Speak!

오디오를 듣고 큰소리로 따라 읽어 보세요.

A 05-3

Elijah: The Man Who Was Fed by Ravens

Elijah means "Yahweh is my God."

When he was a prophet, King Ahab reigned over Israel.

King Ahab worshiped idols,[1] so God was angry at him.

Elijah was sent to King Ahab to deliver God's message.

"There will be no rain or dew[2] in Israel until I say so."

King Ahab wanted to kill Elijah because of this bad news.

God told Elijah to hide from that angry king.

While he stayed in a hiding place, God sent ravens[3] to bring bread and meat to him.

He drank water from the stream.[4]

After three years of hiding, God ordered Elijah to go to King Ahab and give rain to dry lands.

God sent Elijah to the widow[5] who had little food to eat.

He multiplied[6] her food according to[7] God's order, and she treated him well with that food.

He also revived[8] her son.

Elijah hit the Jordan River with his coat, and it parted.[9]

When he walked with Elisha, a chariot[10] of fire took him into the heaven.

Words and Idioms Consult the index dictionary if needed.

1 **idol**

picture or statue that is worshipped as a god 우상

2 **dew**

3 **raven**

4 **stream**

5 **widow**

6 **multiply**

7 **according to**

8 **revive**

9 **part**

10 **chariot**

B 05-4

Jezebel: The Wife of King Ahab

JezebeI was queen of Israel and wife of King Ahab.

She was notorious[1] as the queen who adored and worshiped the pagan[2] god, Baal.

The lands of Israel became dry after Elijah came and delivered God's message that it would not rain for a long time.

Jezebel believed that her god would answer first when Elijah came back and asked her and her priests[3] to choose the true God who answered by fire.

To her surprise, Baal did not answer when the 450 priests called on[4] their god all day.

They even cut themselves with swords, but there was no answer.

Contrary to[5] her expectation, Elijah's God started a fire even though the altar[6] was wet with water.

After witnessing[7] this, the people of Israel bowed down and worshiped Elijah's God as their one true God.

Immediately it rained again.

Jezebel was so furious[8] that she sent Elijah a message that he would die like her priests.

But she could not kill him because he ran away and was led by God.

Words and Idioms Consult the index dictionary if needed.

1 **notorious**

famous for something bad 악명 높은

2 **pagan**

3 **priest**

4 **call on**

5 **contrary to**

6 **altar**

7 **witness**

8 **furious**

Think about It! Who is Elijah? Who is Jezebel?

Grammar Points

현재완료 시제 (Present Perfect Tense) ❷

현재완료 시제는 과거의 어느 한 순간부터 현재 말하는 순간까지 어떤 일을 계속하거나 끝냈다는 것을 나타낸다고 지난 과에서 공부했습니다. 그리고 대표적인 용법으로 말하는 시점까지 경험한 것에 대해 이야기하는 것을 먼저 익혀봤죠. 이번 과에서는 현재완료 시제의 용법 중 '완료'에 대해 살펴보도록 하죠.

❶ 일의 '완료'를 나타내는 현재완료: have/has (just) + p.p. (막) ~했다

과거의 어느 한 순간에 시작했던 일을 현재 이 시점에서 끝냈을 때도 현재완료를 씁니다. 특히 just와 함께 쓰면 '막' 완료했다는 어감이 강해지죠.

I **have just finished** my homework. 난 막 숙제를 끝냈어요.

❷ 현재완료와 단순과거 시제

현재완료 시제 중 '완료' 용법은 단순과거 시제로 나타낼 수도 있습니다. 단순과거 시제 역시 끝난 일을 말하기 때문이죠.

I **have just finished** my homework. 난 막 숙제를 끝냈어요.

I **just finished** my homework. 난 막 숙제를 끝냈어요.

Exercise 다음 우리말을 현재완료 시제와 단순과거 시제를 모두 사용해 영어로 써 보세요.

1 우리는 방금 점심을 먹었다.

(현재완료) ______________________

(단순과거) ______________________

2 엄마는 이미 전화를 끊으셨다. (already, hang up the phone)

(현재완료) ______________________

(단순과거) ______________________

Let's Talk!

A Let's Memorize the Patterns. 05-5

message 전갈, 메시지

message의 가장 대표적인 의미는 '전갈'로, 요새는 우리말로도 그냥 '메시지'라 표현하는 게 일반적이죠. 휴대폰 문자도 message란 단어를 이용해 text message라고 합니다.

Elijah delivered God's **message** to King Ahab.
엘리야는 아합 왕에게 하나님의 전갈을 전했다.

I'd like to leave a **message**, please.
메모를 남기고 싶은데요.

I'll send you a **text message**. / I'll **text** you.
문자할게요.

B Let's Talk: Pair Work

다음은 핸드폰 관련 대화입니다. 큰 소리로 읽어본 후, 두 명씩 짝을 지어 연습해 보세요.

1

Partner A I have to go. I'll send you a **text message** about tomorrow's meeting.

Partner B Okay!

2

Partner A How come you're not answering my call?

Partner B I'm sorry. My phone went dead.

or I'm sorry. I didn't hear the phone ring. I set my volume on soundless/low.

or I'm sorry. I didn't hear the phone ring. I had set it to vibrate.

answer someone's call ~의 전화를 받다 | my phone went dead 폰 배터리가 다 됐다 | on soundless 무음으로 | on low (소리를) 작게 | set it to vibrate 진동으로 설정하다 (여기서 it은 앞에서 언급한 the phone을 가리킴)

Confession & Prayer

A My Confession 05-6

After Elijah heard that the wicked Queen Jezebel wanted to kill him, he ran for dear life to Beersheba, far in the south of Judah. While he went a day's journey into a desert, he sat down under a broom tree and prayed that he might die. Then he lay down under the tree and fell asleep. The angel touched him and gave him food and water. The angel did this for forty days and nights until Elijah reached Horeb, the mountain of God. While he stayed in the cave, he heard the voice of God, "Go, stand on the mountain at attention before God. God will pass by." He saw the powerful wind, earthquake, and a fire coming one by one, but there was no God. Finally he heard the whisper of God to go back the way he came through the desert to Damascus. He decided to follow God's words even though it would take his life. There are times when we want to escape from difficulties like Elijah. As Christians, what should we do when we are in a difficult situation? Share your idea with group members and write down your idea in English if you can.

사악한 왕후 이세벨이 자신을 죽이려 한다는 소식을 듣고 엘리야는 자기의 생명을 위해 유다의 남쪽지방인 브엘세바로 멀리 도망갔습니다. 엘리야는 광야로 들어가 하룻길쯤 가서 한 로뎀 나무 아래에 앉아 자기를 죽게 해달라고 기도했습니다. 그런 후 로뎀 나무 아래에 누워 잠이 들었는데, 천사가 그를 어루만져 깨우고선 음식과 물을 주었죠. 천사는 엘리야가 하나님의 산인 호렙산에 도착할 때까지 40일 동안 밤낮으로 그에게 음식과 물을 주었습니다. 엘리야가 그곳 굴에 들어가 머물 때에 "너는 나가서 여호와 앞에서 산에 서라. 여호와께서 지나가실 것이다."라는 하나님의 음성을 들었습니다. 엘리야는 강한 바람과 지진, 그리고 불이 연달아 지나가는 것을 보았지만 그 안에 하나님은 계시지 아니하였습니다. 마침내 엘리야는 왔던 길을 되돌아 광야를 통해 다메섹에 가라는 하나님의 속삭임을 들었습니다. 엘리야는 목숨을 내놓는 일일지라도 하나님의 말씀을 따르기로 결심했습니다. 우리에게도 엘리야처럼 어려움에서 벗어나고 싶은 때가 있습니다. 그리스도인으로서 이렇게 어려운 상황에 처했을 때 우리는 어떻게 행동해야 할까요? 다른 친구들과 이야기를 나누어 본 후 여러분의 생각을 가능하면 영어로 써보세요.

영어로 쓰기가 힘들다면 우리말로 써도 괜찮습니다.

B Elijah's Prayer 05-7

하나님께 비를 보내달라고 엘리야는 갈멜 산꼭대기(the top of Carmel)에 올라가서 땅에 꿇어 엎드려(bent down to the ground) 그의 얼굴을 무릎 사이에 넣고(put his face between his knees) 간절히 기도하였습니다. (1 Kings 18:42) 바알의 제사장들 앞에서 번제물을 놓고 드린 엘리야의 기도를 읽으며 그가 얼마나 절실하게 또 믿음을 갖고 기도했는지 생각해 보세요.

O LORD, God of Abraham, Isaac and Israel, let it be known today that you are God in Israel and that I am your servant and have done all these things at your command.

Answer me, O LORD, answer me, so these people will know that you, O LORD, are God, and that you are turning their hearts back again.

(1 Kings 18:36-37)

아브라함과 이삭과 이스라엘의 하나님 여호와여, 주께서 이스라엘 중에서 하나님이신 것과 내가 주의 종인 것과 내가 주의 말씀대로 이 모든 일을 행하는 것을 오늘 알게 하옵소서.

여호와여, 내게 응답하옵소서, 내게 응답하옵소서, 이 백성에게 주 여호와는 하나님이신 것과 주는 그들의 마음을 되돌이키심을 알게 하옵소서.

(열왕기상 18:36-37)

Write a Prayer for Yourself!

엘리야의 기도문을 외워보는 건 어떨까요? 다 외운 다음엔 직접 한번 써보세요.

O Lord,

A Poem & Song

Elijah the Tishbite

(to the tune 'Michael Finnegan')

Ahab, son of Omri, King of Israel,
had for a wife, a queen called Jezebel.
Both turned from God
to an idol called Ba-al.
King Ahab and Jezebel of Israel
did rebel.

Elijah the Tishbite, from Tishbe in Gilead,
he was a prophet, who made them very mad!
"God will send a drought,
with no rain to be had!"
said the Tishbite from Tishbe in Gilead,
very sad!

In the Wadi Cherith, east of the Jordan,
Elijah hid from this man and his woman.
The ravens fed him in the
evening and the morning
In the Wadi Cherith of the Jordan,
it wasn't fun!

Later he left for a town, named Zarephath,
there he saved a widow's son from death.
Fed them, and their thirst Elijah quenched.
In Zarephath town where he did rest,
being a guest.

Then back he went to a mount name Carmel;
faced the king, overcame his prophets. Well,
so I'm told, the people turned to God again,
and the clouds returned and the rain it fell,
at Carmel!

used with permission www.sheilahamil.co.uk

06

The Bald Prophet

The company of the prophets from Jericho, who were watching, said, "The spirit of Elijah is resting on Elisha." And they went to meet him and bowed to the ground before him. (2 Kings 2:15)

Who Am I?

STEP 1 Listen!

오디오를 듣고 말하고 있는 인물이 누구인지 알아맞혀 보세요.

A

06-1

Who am I?

Script

A

My name means 'God is salvation.' I was bald. I was chosen by God to be Elijah's helper while I was plowing a field. Elijah and I traveled together, telling many people about God's love. While I was with Elijah, I saw a fiery chariot pulled by fiery horses coming down from the sky. It separated us and took Elijah into heaven. At that time, Elijah's coat fell down. I struck the water with it and the water parted. After that, I took his place as God's prophet.

I multiplied the oil of the woman who owed a lot of money. She would be deprived of her two sons, sold as slaves, if she did not pay her debt.

A friendly couple of Shunem built a room for me in their house. They helped me do God's work. I prayed for them to have a baby, so God gave them a beautiful baby boy.

After I was dead, touching my bones brought a dead man back to life. (2 Kings 13:20-21)
Who am I?

B

06-2

Who am I?

Script

B

I was a great army commander of the king of Aram. I was brave, but I had a terrible skin disease called leprosy.

One day, my wife asked me to go and see the prophet in Samaria. She believed that prophet would heal my leprosy. So I reached his home, but I could not see him. I only got a message from his man: "Go, wash yourself seven times in the Jordan, and your flesh will be restored and you will be cleansed." I was angry at this message, but my servant persuaded me to do it. So I dipped myself in the Jordan River, and I found out that my skin disease was gone! I was so happy that I ran to thank him for curing my disease. This miracle made me believe the God of the Israelites was the only true God! Who am I?

STEP 2 Speak!

오디오를 듣고 큰소리로 따라 읽어 보세요.

A 06-3

Elisha: The Bald Prophet

Elisha means 'God is salvation.'[1]

He was bald.[2]

While plowing[3] a field, he was chosen by God to be Elijah's helper.

Elijah and Elisha traveled together, telling many people about God's love.

While Elisha was with Elijah, he saw a fiery[4] chariot pulled by fiery horses coming down from the sky.

It separated them and took Elijah into heaven.

At that time, Elijah's coat fell down.[5]

Elisha struck the water with it and the water parted.

After that, Elisha took his place[6] as God's prophet.

He multiplied the oil of the woman who owed[7] a lot of money.

She would be deprived[8] of her two sons, sold as slaves,[9] if she did not pay her debt.[10]

A friendly couple of Shunem built a room for Elisha in their house.

They helped him do God's work.

Elisha prayed for them to have a baby, so God gave them a beautiful baby boy.

After Elisha was dead, touching his bones brought a dead man back to life. (2 Kings 13:20-21)

Words and Idioms Consult the index dictionary if needed.

1 **salvation**
the act of being saved by God from evil 구원

2 **bald**

3 **plow**

4 **fiery**

5 **fall down**

6 **take someone's place**

7 **owe**

8 **deprive**

9 **slave**

10 **debt**

B 06-4

Naaman: Great Commander Who Had a Terrible Skin Disease

Naaman was a great army commander[1] of the king of Aram.
He was brave, but he had a terrible skin disease called leprosy.[2]

One day, Naaman's wife asked him to go and see Elisha, the prophet, in Samaria.
She believed that Elisha would heal[3] her husband's leprosy.
So Naaman reached Elisha's home, but he could not see the prophet.
He only got a message from Elisha's man:
"Go, wash yourself seven times in the Jordan, and your flesh[4] will be restored[5] and you will be cleansed."
Naaman was angry at this message, but his servant persuaded[6] him to do it.
So he dipped[7] himself in the Jordan River, and he found out that his skin disease was gone!
Naaman was so happy that he ran to thank Elisha for curing[8] his disease.
That miracle made him believe the God of the Israelites was the only true God!

Words and Idioms Consult the index dictionary if needed.

1 **commander**

one in an official position of command or control 지휘자

2 **leprosy**

3 **heal**

4 **flesh**

5 **restore**

6 **persuade**

7 **dip**

8 **cure**

Think about It! Who is Elisha? Who is Naaman?

Grammar Points

현재완료 시제 (Present Perfect Tense) ❸

지금까지 현재완료 시제의 용법 중 경험과 완료에 대해 살펴봤습니다. 이번 과에서는 현재완료 시제의 '계속적' 용법에 대해 공부해 보도록 하죠.

❶ 일의 '계속'을 나타내는 현재완료: have/has + p.p. 계속 ~했다

과거의 어느 한 순간에 시작했던 행동이나 상태가 말하는 이 순간 이후에도 계속되는 경우, 현재완료를 씁니다.

I **have been** in class since eight o'clock this morning. 아침 8시부터 계속 수업을 듣고 있어.

▶ 말하는 순간 이후에도 수업을 계속 듣고 있을 예정임

We **have known** Myeonghee for three years. 영희를 안 지 3년 됐어.

▶ 말하는 순간 이후에도 아는 상태는 계속될 것임

❷ 현재완료의 계속적 용법이 좋아하는 전치사 for와 since

현재완료 시제의 계속적 용법에서 많이 사용되는 전치사인 for와 since는 시간 개념이 다릅니다. for는 '일정기간'을 나타내는 반면, since는 그 행동이나 일이 '시작되는 첫 순간'을 나타내죠.

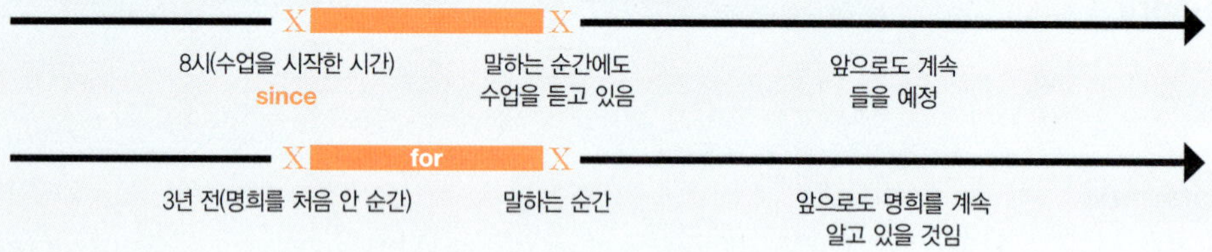

Exercise 다음 우리말을 현재완료 시제를 사용해 영어로 써보세요.

1 난 어렸을 때부터 여기서 살았다.

2 나는 이 자전거를 3년째 갖고 있다.

3 내 남동생은 지난해부터 중국어 공부를 하고 있다. (my younger brother)

Let's Talk!

A Let's Memorize the Patterns. 06-5

reach 연락하다, 도착하다

reach 하면 보통 '도착하다'는 의미로 많이 알고 있죠? 즉 reach 뒤에 목적지가 와서 '~에 도착하다'는 의미로 쓰입니다. 그런데 이 reach는 뒤에 사람을 써서 그 사람에게 '연락하다', 그 사람과 '연락이 닿다'는 의미로도 활용되죠. 주로 전화 연락과 관련해서 많이 쓰입니다.

Where can I **reach** you? 어디로 연락하면 되나요?

You can **reach** me at 02-123-4567. 02-123-4567로 연락주시면 됩니다.

Just tell her that Heesu tried to **reach** her. 희수가 전화했다고 말해주세요.

Naaman **reached** Elisha's home. 나아만은 엘리사의 집에 도착했다.

When will we **reach** the destination? 언제 목적지에 도착할까요?
▶ 비행기나 고속버스를 탔을 때 사용하면 좋겠죠?

B Let's Talk: Pair Work

두 명씩 짝을 지어 다음 대화를 나눠보세요.

1

Partner A Hello, may I speak to Mr. Kim?
Partner B He just stepped out for a moment.
Partner A Is there any other way to **reach** him?
Partner B You can try his cell phone.
Partner A Thank you.

May I speak to ~? ~와 통화할 수 있을까요? | step out for a moment 잠시 나가다 | cell phone 휴대폰

2

Partner A Where can I **reach** ____________?
Partner B You can **reach** ____________ at ____________.

Confession & Prayer

A My Confession 06-6

Naaman was angry when he got a message from a man, not Elisha. He thought that Elisha himself "would surely come to him and stand and call on the name of the LORD his God, wave his hand over the spot and cure him of his leprosy." (2 Kings 5:11) He even said, "Are not Abana and Pharpar, the rivers of Damascus, better than any of the waters of Israel? Couldn't I wash in them and be cleansed?" (2 Kings 5:12) Because he was a high commander of the king of Aram, he thought he deserved to be healed by Elisha himself. What do you think about his reaction after receiving Elisha's message? What made him say that? Share your idea with group members and write down your idea in English if you can.

나아만은 엘리사가 아니라 사자가 전갈을 가져와서 화가 났습니다. 나아만은 엘리사가 직접 "자신에게로 나와 서서 그의 하나님 여호와의 이름을 부르고 그의 손을 그 부위 위에 흔들어 나병을 고쳐줄 것이라"(열왕기하 5:11) 생각했던 거죠. 나아만은 "다메섹 강 아바나와 바르발은 이스라엘 모든 강물보다 낫지 아니하냐? 내가 거기서 몸을 씻으면 깨끗하게 되지 아니하랴?"(열왕기하 5:12) 라고까지 말했습니다. 나아만은 아람 왕의 군대 장관이었기 때문에 마땅히 엘리사의 치료를 직접 받을 만한 자격이 있다고 생각했죠. 엘리사의 전갈을 받은 후 나아만의 행동에 대해 여러분은 어떻게 생각하나요? 왜 그가 그렇게 말했다고 생각하나요? 다른 친구들과 이야기를 나누어 본 후 여러분의 생각을 가능하면 영어로 써보세요.

영어로 쓰기가 힘들다면 우리말로 써도 괜찮습니다.

B Let's Pray! 06-7

엘리사는 죽은 아이를 살려달라는 수넴 여인의 간청을 듣고 죽은 아이가 누워 있는 방으로 들어가 하나님께 기도를 드립니다. 그런 후 "아이 위에 올라 엎드려 자기 입을 그의 입에, 자기 눈을 그의 눈에, 자기 손을 그의 손에 대고 그의 몸에 엎드립니다."(열왕기하 4:34) 그러자 아이의 살이 차차 따뜻해지기 시작합니다. 하나님의 손길이 엘리사를 통해 아이를 살리신 것입니다. 엘리사가 소년의 몸 곳곳에 하나님의 영을 불어 넣는 그 장면을 상상해보며 우리 역시 우리의 눈, 귀, 발, 입술, 손, 마음이 모두 다 하나가 되어 하나님을 섬길 수 있도록 기도해 볼까요?

Two little eyes to look to God;	하나님을 바라보는 두 개의 작은 눈
Two little ears to hear His Word;	하나님의 말씀을 듣는 두 개의 작은 귀
Two little feet to walk in His ways;	하나님의 길을 걷는 두 개의 작은 발
Two little lips to sing His praise;	하나님을 찬양하는 두 개의 작은 입술
Two little hands to do His will;	하나님의 의지를 행하는 두 개의 작은 손
One little heart to love Him still.	여전히 하나님을 사랑하는 하나의 작은 마음

Write a Prayer for Yourself!

이제 위의 기도를 영어로 직접 써보세요.

A Poem & Song

Naaman was a Fighting Man

(to the tune 'Pop Goes the Weasel')

Naaman was a fighting man
and he was a leper.
Took advice when his young maid
(POP)
told him of Elisha.

Elisha told him what to do,
but he wouldn't do it.
He was proud and wouldn't bathe
(POP)
in the river Jordan.

He was angry, but his friends
persuaded him to do it.
So he bathed and he was cured
(POP)
just as the prophet told him.

To the prophet he returned,
to show him he was grateful.
Elisha would not take his gift
(POP)
not even a plateful.

"Then I will serve no other god!"
said Naaman to Elisha.
"Go in peace," the prophet said.
(POP)
"Yes, I believe ya!"

Elisha's servant heard all this;
the greedy rogue, Gehazi,
who followed Naaman, claimed the gift
(POP)
and became a LEPER!

used with permission www.sheilahamil.co.uk

07

The Teacher Well Versed in the Law of Moses

With praise and thanksgiving they sang to the LORD:

"He is good; his love to Israel endures forever." (Ezra 3:11)

Who Am I?

STEP 1 Listen!

오디오를 듣고 말하고 있는 인물이 누구인지 알아맞혀 보세요.

A

07-1

Who am I?

Script

A

I was a priest and descendant of Aaron. I lived during the time the Israelites began to return from exile. I knew a lot of the teachings of Moses, so King Artaxerxes sent me to Israel to teach the people how to live God's way.

Many of the families that had been in exile in Babylon returned with me to Israel. For the people who assembled in the square before the Water Gate, I read and gave the meaning of the verses written in the Book of the Law of God. Through this, I helped the Israelites repent of their sins and relearn their faith. Who am I?

B

07-2

Who am I?

Script

B

I was a cupbearer for King Artaxerxes in Babylon. I got permission from the King to return to Jerusalem after I heard the news that the great wall of Jerusalem was broken down and needed repair.

I was appointed a governor of Jerusalem. After I returned to my hometown, I encouraged my people to rebuild the walls. They agreed and began to work, but many of the kingdoms surrounding my home place devised many plots to stop this building. However, I always believed God would help me. I prayed continuously and God answered my prayer. It took only 52 days to rebuild the walls.

I also saw my people suffering from debts and land mortgages, so I canceled all of them. I also refused to take a salary as a governor. I was a governor for twelve years. Who am I?

STEP 2 Speak!

오디오를 듣고 큰소리로 따라 읽어 보세요.

A 07-3

Ezra: The Teacher Well Versed in the Law of Moses

Ezra was a priest and descendant[1] of Aaron.

He lived during the time the Israelites began to return from exile.[2]

Ezra knew a lot of the teachings[3] of Moses, so King Artaxerxes sent[4] him to Israel to teach the people how to live God's way.

Many of the families that had been in exile in Babylon returned with him to Israel.

For the people who assembled[5] in the square before the Water Gate, Ezra read and gave the meaning of the verses[6] written in the Book of the Law of God.

This made the Israelites repent[7] of their sins[8] and helped them relearn[9] their faith.[10]

Words and Idioms Consult the index dictionary if needed.

1 **descendant**

a relative of a person who lived in the past 후손

2 **exile**

3 **teachings**

4 **send**

5 **assemble**

6 **verse**

7 **repent**

8 **sin**

9 **relearn**

10 **faith**

B 07-4

Nehemiah: Righteous Governor of Jerusalem

Nehemiah was a cupbearer[1] for King Artaxerxes in Babylon.
He got permission[2] from the King to return to Jerusalem after he heard the news that the great wall of Jerusalem was broken down and needed repair.

Nehemiah was appointed[3] a governor[4] of Jerusalem.
After he returned to Jerusalem, he encouraged the Israelites to[5] rebuild the walls.
They agreed and began to work, but many of the kingdoms surrounding Jerusalem devised[6] many plots[7] to stop this building.
However, Nehemiah always believed God would help him.
He prayed continuously and God answered his prayer.
It took only 52 days to rebuild the walls.

Nehemiah also saw the Israelites suffering from the debts and land mortgages,[8] so he canceled all of debts and mortgages.
He also refused to take a salary as a governor.
Nehemiah was a governor for twelve years.

Words and Idioms Consult the index dictionary if needed.

1 **cupbearer**

someone who carries a drinking cup for a king 술 관원

2 **permission**

3 **appoint**

4 **governor**

5 **encourage someone to do**

6 **devise**

7 **plot**

8 **mortgage**

Think about It! Talk about Ezra and Nehemiah. Who are they?

Grammar Points

과거완료 시제 (Past Perfect Tense)

과거완료 시제(had + p.p.)는 대과거라고도 합니다. 과거보다 더 이전의 시제를 말하고 싶을 때 쓰는 시제입니다. 다음의 그림과 예문을 보며 과거완료 시제의 쓰임을 살펴보도록 하죠.

When Suji **arrived** at the cafe, Minsu **wasn't** there. He **had left**.
수지가 카페에 도착했을 때 민수는 거기 없었다. 민수는 떠난 상태였다.

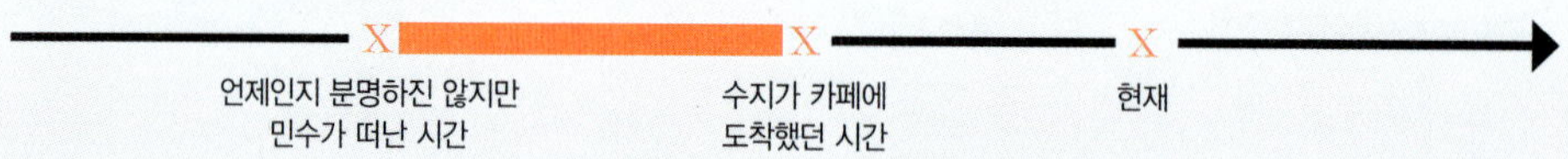

▶ 과거에 수지가 도착했던 시간보다 민수가 먼저 떠났으므로 대과거(had left)를 씀

King Joash **found** that the temple of the LORD **had been damaged** a lot.
요아스 왕은 하나님의 성전이 많이 손상된 것을 발견했다.

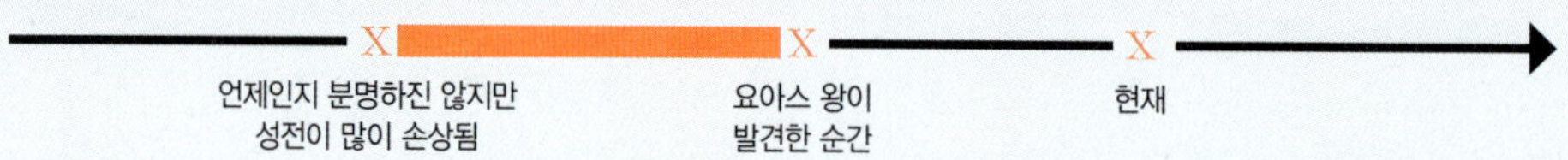

▶ 요아스 왕이 발견한 순간보다 성전이 손상된 것이 먼저 있었던 일이므로 대과거(had been damaged)를 씀

Exercise 주어진 동사를 과거와 과거완료 중 적절한 시제로 바꿔 빈칸을 채워보세요.

1 난 희수를 찾았지만 그 애는 교실을 나가고 없었다.

I ______________ (look for) Heesu, but she ______________ (leave) the classroom.

2 내가 도착했을 때 할머니는 안 계셨다. 할머니는 막 외출하셨다.

Grandma ______________ (not, be) home when I arrived. She ______________ (just, go out).

3 난 지난 목요일에 영희를 만났다. 3년 동안 영희를 죽 보지 못했었는데 말이다.

I ______________ (meet) Yeonghee last Thursday. I ______________ (not, see) her for three years.

Let's Talk!

A Let's Memorize the Patterns. 07-5

It takes + 기간 ~가 걸린다

- It takes + 기간 + to + 동사원형 …하는 데 ~가 걸린다
- It takes + 기간 + for A to + 동사원형 A가 …하는 데 ~가 걸린다

take에는 시간이 얼마나 '걸린다'라는 의미가 있어서 어떤 일을 하는 데 걸린 시간이나 기간을 나타낼 때 위와 같은 형태로 곧잘 쓰입니다.

A: How long will it take? 얼마나 걸릴까요?
B: **It will take** about ten minutes. 10분 정도 걸릴 거예요.

It took only 52 days **to** rebuild the temple.
성전을 다시 짓는 데 52일밖에 걸리지 않았다.

It's taking too long **for** the soap opera **to** start.
(시작하기 전에 광고가 너무 많아서) 연속극을 시작하는 데 너무 오래 걸려요.

B Let's Talk: Pair Work

두 명씩 짝을 지어 다음 대화를 나눠보세요. 그런 다음 Substitute Drills에 주어진 표현을 이용해 응용해 보세요.

1

Partner A I came here by subway.
Partner B You did? How long did it take (to get here)?
Partner A **It took** about one hour.

Substitute Drills (1) by bus - thirty minutes (2) by taxi - fifteen minutes

2

Partner A Tom just finished reading that book.
Partner B He did? How long did it take?
Partner A **It took** him about a week to finish it.

Substitute Drills (1) doing his homework - two hours (2) doing his laundry - one and half hour

Confession & Prayer

A My Confession 07-6

When Nehemiah looked at the broken walls and burned gates of Jerusalem, he figured out how big the job was and how long it would take. He firmly believed that God would help him and the Israelites, so he encouraged the people to rebuild the walls. They began to work, but the enemies devised many plots to stop this working. So each day, half the men worked and half kept enemies away. The Israelites believed God was with them, so they worked together without fear. As a result, the wall was finished in 52 days. There are times when we should work together. If you find someone who does not want to corporate with the others, how can you make him work with everyone? Share your idea with group members and write down your idea in English if you can.

느헤미야가 예루살렘의 부서진 성벽과 불탄 성문을 바라보았을 때 이 일이 얼마나 대단한 일이고 얼마나 오래 걸릴 일인지 생각했습니다. 그는 하나님이 그와 이스라엘 사람들을 도와줄 것이라 굳건히 믿었기 때문에 이스라엘 백성들에게 용기를 주어 벽을 고치도록 했습니다. 이스라엘 백성들은 일을 시작했지만 적들은 여러 가지 흉계를 써서 그 일을 막으려고 했습니다. 그래서 매일 사람들 반은 일을 했고 반은 적을 물리쳤습니다. 이들은 하나님이 자신들과 함께하심을 믿었기 때문에 두려움 없이 일을 했습니다. 그 결과 성벽 수리는 52일 만에 끝났습니다. 우리가 함께 일을 해야만 하는 경우가 있습니다. 만약 여러분이 다른 사람들과 함께 일하기를 원하지 않는 사람을 본다면, 그가 어떻게 함께 일하도록 할 수 있을까요? 다른 친구들과 이야기를 나누어 본 후 여러분의 생각을 가능하면 영어로 써보세요.

영어로 쓰기가 힘들다면 우리말로 써도 괜찮습니다.

B Let's Pray! 07-7

예루살렘의 성벽이 파괴되고 성문이 불탔다는 소식을 들은 느헤미야는 울었습니다. 그곳에 가서 사람들을 돕고 싶었지만 왕의 허락 없이는 갈 수 없었습니다. 그래서 느헤미야는 하나님께 기도를 했습니다.

O Lord, let your ear be attentive to the prayer of this your servant and to the prayer of your servants who delight in revering your name. Give your servant success today by granting him favor in the presence of this man.

(Nehemiah 1:11)

주여 구하오니 귀를 기울이사 종의 기도와 주의 이름을 경외하기를 기뻐하는 종들의 기도를 들으시고 오늘 종이 형통하여 이 사람 앞에서 은혜를 입게 하옵소서.

(느헤미야 1:11)

Write a Prayer for Yourself!

위의 기도문을 외워보는 건 어떨까요? 다 외운 다음엔 직접 한번 써보세요. 그리고 여러분도 어떤 일을 이루고자 할 때 이 기도문을 이용해 하나님께 기도해 보세요.

O Lord,

Ezra the Scribe

(to the tune 'Miss Polly Had a Dolly')

Now Ezra was a scribe,
who read the 'Book of Law.'
Taught the people all
they'd never heard before.
He read it from the dawn
until the noon day sun;
with his little team of helpers,
t'was a Marathon!

And as the people heard it
they began to cry.
Listen very carefully
and I'll tell you why.
The people had been 'exiled',
didn't know they'd sinned.
Said Ezra, "Go and dry your eyes
and come back again."

For seven long days
the holy word was read.
I bet they thought about it
even in their beds.
And so they decided
all of them as one,
that they would all repent
before the day was done!

used with permission www.sheilahamil.co.uk

08

The Brave Queen Who Saved the Jews

And who knows but that you have come to royal position for such a time as this?

(Esther 4:14)

Who Am I?

STEP 1 Listen!

오디오를 듣고 말하고 있는 인물이 누구인지 알아맞혀 보세요.

A

08-1

Who am I?

Script

A

I was an orphan. I lived in the land of Persia with my older cousin. I was very beautiful so I was chosen as a queen. My husband, King Xerxes, did not know I was a Jew because my old cousin forbade me from telling it.

Haman, the king's prime minister, hated the Jewish people. He made a vicious plan to kill all of them. After hearing about this, my old cousin sent me a message to go to the king and beg him to save our people. I invited my husband and Haman to a special dinner. At the dinner I told the king about Haman's vicious plan and asked him to save my people. The king accepted my requests. Haman was killed and my old cousin became a new prime minister. After that, the Jewish people could live safely and happily. Who am I?

B

08-2

Who am I?

Script

B

I was a Jew, but I had a beautiful cousin who became a queen of the Persian king, Xerxes. I happened to overhear two Persian officials' plan to kill the king. I prevented it by reporting their plan to the queen. By virtue of this, I was honored by the king.

I was about to be hanged by Haman because I refused to bow down to him, but the king's honoring of me saved my life. Haman, the vicious prime minister, tried to kill all the Jewish people. I told this to the queen and convinced her to go to the king and save the Jews. My cousin was brave enough to tell the king about Haman's vicious plan. After Haman was killed, I became a prime minister. I became powerful and famous enough to keep my people safe. Who am I?

STEP 2 Speak!

오디오를 듣고 큰소리로 따라 읽어 보세요.

A 08-3

Esther: The Brave Queen Who Saved the Jews

Esther was an orphan.[1]

She lived in the land of Persia with her older cousin, Mordecai.

Esther was very beautiful, so she was chosen as a queen.

King Xerxes did not know she was a Jew[2] because Mordecai forbade her from[3] telling it.

Haman, the king's prime minister,[4] hated the Jewish people.

He made a vicious[5] plan to kill all of them.

After hearing about this, Mordecai sent her a message to go to the king and beg him to[6] save her people.

Esther invited the king and Haman to[7] a special dinner.

At the dinner she told the king about Haman's vicious plan and asked him to[8] save her people.

The king accepted[9] her requests.[10]

Haman was killed and Mordecai became a new prime minister.

After that, the Jewish people could live safely and happily.

Words and Idioms Consult the index dictionary if needed.

1 **orphan**

a child whose parents have died 고아

2 **Jew**

3 **forbid someone from doing**

4 **prime minister**

5 **vicious**

6 **beg someone to do**

7 **invite someone to**

8 **ask someone to do**

9 **accept**

10 **request**

B 08-4

Mordecai: The Jewish Man to Be Honoured by a Persian King

Mordecai was a Jew, but he had a beautiful cousin who became a queen of the Persian king, Xerxes.

One day, Mordecai happened to[1] overhear[2] two Persian officials'[3] plan to kill the king.

He saved the king's life by reporting[4] their plan to the queen.

By virtue of[5] this, Mordecai was honored by the king.

At that time, Mordecai was about to be hanged[6] by Haman because he refused to[7] bow down to[8] him, but the king's honoring of him saved his life.

Haman, the vicious prime minister, tried to kill all of the Jewish people.

Mordecai told this to the queen and convinced[9] her to go to the king and save the Jews.

The queen was brave enough to tell the king about Haman's vicious plan.

After Haman was killed, Mordecai became a prime minister.

He became powerful and famous enough to keep[10] his people safe.

Words and Idioms Consult the index dictionary if needed.

1 **happen to do**

to do something by chance 우연히 ~하다

2 **overhear**

3 **official**

4 **report**

5 **by virtue of**

6 **hang**

7 **refuse to do**

8 **bow down to someone**

9 **convince**

10 **keep**

Grammar Points

동사의 현재형, 현재분사형, 과거(분사)형

일반적으로 동사의 현재형, 현재분사형, 과거형, 과거분사형은 일정한 규칙에 따라 변화합니다. 이러한 동사를 규칙동사라고 하며, 이 장에서는 이 규칙에 관해 공부해 보겠습니다.

❶ 주어가 3인칭 단수일 때 일반동사의 현재형 만들기

기본	동사원형+s	I like → He/She likes
y로 끝나는 동사	-y → -ies	I study → He/She studies

▶ play처럼 y 바로 앞에 모음(발음상 a, e, i, o, u)이 오는 경우엔 He plays처럼 그냥 -s만 붙임

❷ 일반동사의 현재분사형 만들기

기본	동사원형+ing	sing → singing	cook → cooking
모음 e로 끝나는 동사	-e → -ing	smile → smiling	hope → hoping
(한 음절 동사) 자음+모음+자음	자음+모음+자음+자음 +ing	stop → stopping	plan → planning
(두 음절 이상) 강세모음+자음으로 끝나는 동사	마지막 자음+자음 +ing	prefer → preferring cf. visit → visiting	admit → admitting offer → offering
모음 ie로 끝나는 동사	-ie → -ying	die → dying	lie → lying

❸ 일반동사의 과거(분사)형 만들기

기본	동사원형+ed	walk → walked	play → played
모음 e로 끝나는 동사	동사원형+d	smile → smiled	
자음+y로 끝나는 동사	-y → -ied	study → studied cf. pray → prayed	try → tried enjoy → enjoyed
(한 음절 동사) 자음+모음+자음	자음+모음+자음+자음 +ed	plan → planned	stop → stopped
(두 음절 이상) 강세모음+자음으로 끝나는 동사	마지막 자음+자음 +ing	prefer → preferred cf. visit → visited	admit → admitted offer → offered

Let's Talk!

A Let's Memorize the Patterns. 08-5

be about to 막 ~하려고 하다

일반적으로 be about to는 막 뭔가를 하려고 하는 참이라고 할 때 쓰는 관용구입니다. to 뒤에는 동사원형을 쓰죠.

The plane **is about to** land. 비행기가 이제 착륙하려 한다.

▶ 주로 착륙하기 직전에 쓰이는 말입니다.

A: The sun **is about to** set. 해가 지려고 하고 있어요. (가야할 때를 말할 때)

B: Yeah, I better let you go. 네. 보내드려야겠네요.

B Let's Talk: Pair Work

두 명씩 짝을 지어 다음 대화를 나눠보세요. 그런 다음 Substitute Drills에 주어진 표현을 이용해 응용해 보세요.

1

Partner A How come you never replied to the text message ?

Partner B I **was just about to** reply it .

▶ 어째서(How come) 문자 메시지(text message)에 답을 안 해줬냐고 불평하는 말에 막 답하려던 참이었다고 대답하는 대화. 이때 I was just about to ~처럼 be동사를 과거 시제로 쓰는 것에 주의하세요.

Substitute Drills

(1) called me - give you a call (2) gave me an answer - answer you

Confession & Prayer

A My Confession 08-6

Esther got a message from Mordecai. “Go to the king and beg him to help our people.” At first, she refused to do it because she did not want to be put to death. But Mordecai sent her his second message which reminded her of her duty as God’s servant. After fasting and praying for three days, Esther overcame her fear of death. She put on her royal robes and stood before the king without fear. Because of this brave behaviour, Esther could save herself and her people from Haman’s vicious plan to kill all the Jewish people. Sometimes we can meet the situation where we should be brave. If you are in this situation, what are you going to do? Share your idea with group members and write down your idea in English if you can.

에스더는 모르드개에게서 “왕에게 나아가서 그에게 우리 민족을 도와달라고 간청하라”는 전갈을 받았습니다. 처음에 에스더는 죽고 싶지 않았기 때문에 이 일을 하지 않으려 했습니다. 하지만 모르드개는 두 번째 전갈을 보내 하나님의 종으로서 에스더의 의무에 대해 상기시켰습니다. 3일간 금식 기도를 한 후 에스더는 죽음의 공포를 이겨냈습니다. 에스더는 왕후의 예복을 입고 두려움 없이 왕 앞에 섰습니다. 이 용감한 행동 때문에 에스더는 모든 유대인을 죽이려는 하만의 사악한 계획에서부터 자신과 자신의 민족을 구할 수 있었습니다. 때때로 우리는 용감해야만 하는 상황을 만납니다. 만약 이런 상황에 처한다면 여러분은 어떻게 할 건가요? 다른 친구들과 이야기를 나누어 본 후 여러분의 생각을 가능하면 영어로 써보세요.

영어로 쓰기가 힘들다면 우리말로 써도 괜찮습니다.

B Let's Pray! 08-7

다음은 나를 포함하여 우리 가족 모두를 보호해달라는 전통적인 기도입니다. 이번 주에는 잠자리에 들기 전 나의 가족들을 위해 이 영어 기도문을 낭독해 볼까요?

O blessed Lord, protect me please
And my dear parents graciously;
Let your strong arm be ever near
To brothers and to sisters dear.
And all our loved ones in the land,
Shield them with Your own right hand.

오 축복받은 주님, 제발 저를 지켜주세요.
제 사랑하는 부모님도 은총을 내려 지켜주세요.
주님의 강한 팔이 가깝게 가도록 해주세요.
사랑하는 형제와 자매들에게요.
이 땅에서 우리가 사랑하는 모든 사람들을
주님의 오른 팔로 지켜주세요.

Write a Prayer for Yourself!

위의 기도문을 외워보세요. 다 외운 다음엔 직접 한번 써보세요.

O blessed Lord,

A Poem & Song

Good Queen Esther

(to the tune 'London's Burning')

verse two sung in a round

Good Queen Esther by tradition,
won a beauty competition.
And her nation won salvation,
through her prayers and her petition.

Good Queen Esther by tradition,
won a beauty competition.
And her nation won salvation,
through her prayers and her petition.

used with permission www.sheilahamil.co.uk

09

Very Rich Man Who Lived in the Land of Uz

I know that my Redeemer lives, and that in the end he will stand upon the earth.

(Job 19:25)

Who Am I?

STEP 1 Listen!

오디오를 듣고 말하고 있는 인물이 누구인지 알아맞혀 보세요.

A

09-1

Who am I?

Script

A

I was a good and righteous man. I was very wealthy and faithful to God. But suddenly I lost all of my properties and children. Moreover, my entire body was covered with sores. Nevertheless, I remained faithful to God.

One day, three close friends of mine came to comfort me, but their sitting without any word caused me to curse the day I was born. Then, they said that I must have sinned and offended God, but I continued to defend myself and God. Finally God appeared and told me that there were things that men and women could not understand, things that only God could know. I asked forgiveness from God. God forgave me and made me well again. Who am I?

B

09-2

Who am I?

Script

B

I was always roaming the earth, tempting God's people to do evil. One day I visited the kingdom of heaven, and talked about my work on earth with God. When God told me about His faithful servant who hated evil, I was driven by a strong desire to tempt him and make him turn away from Him. So I responded, "He only loves You because You protect his family and You've made him very rich. Take that away and he'll hate You!" God gave me permission to test that man without giving harm to him.

I tested him by making him lose all of his properties and children. I also put him to the test by giving him sores over his entire body. But he did not blame God. He remained faithful to Him. It was very surprising that there was an earthly man who overcame my tests! Who am I?

STEP 2 Speak!

오디오를 듣고 큰소리로 따라 읽어 보세요.

A 09-3

Job: Very Rich Man Who Lived in the Land of Uz

Job was a good and righteous[1] man.

He was very wealthy and faithful[2] to God.

But suddenly he lost all of his properties[3] and children.

Moreover, his entire[4] body was covered with sores.[5]

Nevertheless, Job remained faithful to God.

One day, three close friends came to comfort Job, but their sitting without any word caused him to curse[6] the day he was born.

Then, they said that Job must have sinned[7] and offended[8] God, but he continued to defend[9] himself and God.

Finally God appeared and told Job that there were things that men and women could not understand, things that only God could know.

Job asked forgiveness from God.

God forgave[10] Job and made him well again.

Words and Idioms Consult the index dictionary if needed.

1 **righteous**
morally good or correct, especially according to standards set by religion 정의로운

2 **faithful**

3 **property**

4 **entire**

5 **sore**

6 **curse**

7 **sin**

8 **offend**

9 **defend**

10 **forgive**

B 09-4

Satan: The Tempter of God's People to Do Evil

Satan was always roaming[1] the earth, tempting[2] God's people to do evil.

One day Satan visited the kingdom of heaven, and talked about his work on earth with God.

When God told Satan about His faithful servant Job who hated evil, Satan was driven[3] by a strong desire[4] to tempt Job and make him turn away from[5] God.

So Satan responded, "He only loves You because You protect his family and You've made him very rich. Take that away[6] and he'll hate You!"

God gave Satan the permission[7] to test Job without giving harm to him.

Satan tested Job by making him lose all of his properties and children.

Satan also put him to the test by giving him sores over his entire body.

But Job did not blame[8] God.

He remained faithful to God.

Satan might have been surprised to discover that there was an earthly[9] man who overcame[10] Satan's tests!

Words and Idioms Consult the index dictionary if needed.

1 **roam**

to move or travel with no particular purpose 배회하다

2 **tempt**

3 **drive**

4 **desire**

5 **turn away from**

6 **take away**

7 **permission**

8 **blame**

9 **earthly**

10 **overcome**

Grammar Points

수동형 문장 (Passive Sentences) ❶

주어가 어떤 행동이나 동작을 할 때는 능동형 문장을, 주어가 어떤 행동이나 동작의 대상이 될 때는 수동형 문장을 씁니다. 이번 과에서는 능동형 문장과 비교해 수동형 문장을 살펴보도록 하죠.

❶ 능동형 문장(Active Sentences)과 수동형 문장(Passive Sentences)

일반적으로 능동형 문장이 가장 많이 쓰입니다. 그러나 목적어를 강조하고 싶을 때는 다음과 같이 목적어를 맨 앞 주어 자리로 뺀 수동형 문장을 씁니다. 다음 예문에서 능동형 문장은 기름을 부은 사람이 사무엘임을 말하는 일반적 문장입니다. 하지만 수동형 문장은 사무엘에게 기름 부음을 입은 사람이 바로 젊은 다윗임을 강조하는 문장입니다.

능동형	Samuel	anointed	young David.
	주어	동사	목적어
수동형	Young David	**was anointed**	by Samuel.
	주어	동사(be + 과거분사)	by + 목적어

❷ 수동태로 만들 수 없는 자동사

수동형 문장을 만들 수 있는 동사는 목적어가 있는 타동사임을 기억해 주세요. 자동사는 목적어를 취하지 않기 때문에 수동형 문장을 만들 수 없습니다.

Minjung **came** to my house. 민정이가 우리 집에 왔다.

▶ 목적어가 없으므로 수동형 문장으로 전환할 수 없음

수동태로 만들 수 없는 자동사들							
agree	appear	arrive	become	come	die	go	live
occur	seem	sleep	stand	talk	wait	walk	

Exercise 다음 중 수동형으로 바꿀 수 있는 문장을 찾아 수동형 문장으로 바꿔 써 보세요.

1 My mom made this sweater.
→

2 Alexander Eiffel designed the Eiffel tower.
→

3 Minjung arrived in Seoul last week.
→

Let's Talk!

A Let's Memorize the Patterns. 09-5

must ~인 게 틀림없다 (현재형)
must have + **과거분사** ~였던 게 틀림없다 (과거형)
'~해야만 한다'의 뜻을 가진 조동사 must는 '~인 게 틀림없다'는 의미로도 쓰입니다. 95% 이상의 강한 확신을 나타내죠.

Myeongsu plays soccer every day. He **must** like to play soccer.
명수는 매일 축구를 해. 축구를 좋아하는 게 틀림없어.

A: Was the test hard or what? 시험이 어렵거나 뭐 그랬어?
B: I **must have** failed it. 난 분명히 망쳤어.

B Let's Talk: Pair Work

다음은 전화 통화로, 특히 전화를 잘못 건 상황을 보여주고 있습니다. 두 명씩 짝을 지어 다음 대화를 나눠보세요.

1

Partner A Hyatt Hotel. 하얏트 호텔입니다.

Partner B Oh, I'm sorry. 전화를 잘못 걸었습니다.

전화를 잘못 걸었습니다.
I **must have** dialed the wrong number.
▶ 전화를 잘못 걸었다고 말할 때도 〈must have + 과거분사〉 표현을 쓸 수 있습니다.
I have the wrong number.
It **must** be the wrong number.

Confession & Prayer

A My Confession 09-6

Job lost all of his properties, children and even his health even though he had not sinned. Job's friends believed that his sickness and pain were penalties that God gave for an evil that he had done. Therefore, they argued with him even though Job continued to insist on his sinlessness. His friend Bildad even said to him, "Somewhere, you have forgotten the Lord. So pray that He might forgive you and take away this sickness and pain." There are times when we get hurt by the bad things that our friends say to us. Sometimes we can be hurt by other people who do not like us. When you get hurt by these kinds of things, what are you going to do? Share your idea with group members and write down your idea in English if you can.

욥은 죄를 짓지 않았지만 자신의 재산과 자녀들, 그리고 자신의 건강까지도 모두 잃었습니다. 욥의 친구들은 욥의 질병과 고통이 여호와 하나님께서 그가 행한 사악함에 대한 벌이라 믿었습니다. 그래서 친구들은 비록 욥이 계속 자신은 죄를 짓지 않았다고 주장했지만 그를 비난했습니다. 친구인 빌닷은 욥에게 "어디선가 자네는 여호와 하나님을 잊었을 것이야. 그러니 하나님께 기도하게. 자네를 용서해 주시고 질병과 고통을 없애주기를"이라고 말하기까지 했습니다. 우리는 가끔 친구들이 한 좋지 않은 말들로 상처받습니다. 때로 우리는 우리를 좋아하지 않는 사람들 때문에 상처받기도 합니다. 이런 일로 상처받을 때 여러분은 어떻게 할 건가요? 다른 친구들과 이야기를 나누어 본 후 여러분의 생각을 가능하면 영어로 써보세요.

영어로 쓰기가 힘들다면 우리말로 써도 괜찮습니다.

B Let's Pray! 09-7

다음은 이 세상의 평화와 서로간의 사랑을 구하는 기도문입니다. 큰소리로 읽으며 여러분도 세계 평화와 사랑을 간절히 구해보세요.

Dear Lord, Creator of the world,
Help us to love one another,
Help us care for one another
As sisters or as brothers.
May friendship grow
From nation to nation.
Bring peace to our world
Dear Lord of Creation.

(Anonymous)

이 세상의 창조주이신 사랑의 주님,
우리가 서로 사랑하게 도와주세요.
우리가 서로 돌보게 도와주세요,
형제자매와 같이.
우정이 자라게 해주세요
이 나라에서 저 나라로.
우리의 세상에 평화를 주세요.
사랑하는 창조주 주님.

(익명)

Write a Prayer for Yourself!

위의 기도문을 외워보는 건 어떨까요? 다 외운 다음엔 직접 한번 써보세요.

Dear Lord,

A Poem & Song

Job from Uz

(to the tune 'Do You Know the Muffin Man?')

Do you know a man called Job?
Honest man, pots of dough.
Even owned a big chateau,
and he lived in the land of Uz.
And he lived in the land of Uz.

Satan wandered round the globe,
said to God he oughta know,
Job would curse him if brought low.
This man from the land of Uz.
This man from the land of Uz.

"Go ahead then!" God said, "No,
he won't waver, he will grow!"
Gave the devil leave to go,
and test the man from Uz.
And test the man from Uz.

Soon Job had nothing left to show,
Lost it all, was touch and go!
Vile diseases said 'Hello!'
to the faithful man from Uz.
To the faithful man from Uz.

Not one word against the Lord,
did Job speak to his friends & co.
So God told Satan he must go,
and leave the man from Uz.
And leave the man from Uz.

Now Job's trials all were o'er.
God just blessed him more and more.
All his wealth did God restore
in the merry merry land of Uz.
In the merry merry land of Uz.
In the merry merry land of Uz.

used with permission www.sheilahamil.co.uk

10

The Prophet Who Saw the Future

Do not be afraid, for I am with you; I will bring your children from the east and gather you from the west. (Isaiah 43:5)

Who Am I?

STEP 1 Listen!

오디오를 듣고 말하고 있는 인물이 누구인지 알아맞혀 보세요.

A

10-1

Who am I?

Script

A

My name means "Yahweh is my Salvation." I was known as one of the greatest prophets of Israel. I proclaimed God's coming judgements on Israel and upon the whole earth. Especially, I criticized the kings of Israel for their arrogance and hypocrisy. I also told the Jewish people to repent of their sins, and have faith and follow the Lord even when His ways were not clear to them. I kept saying that God loved and cared for them even though they did not deserve to be loved by God.

I wrote many words about the coming Messiah, and because of this I was called the prophet who saw the future. Who am I?

B

10-2

Who am I?

Script

B

I was a prophet whose nickname was "the weeping prophet." I was consecrated by God before I was born, so I was called to preach when I was very young. God forbade me to marry and have sons and daughters because only disasters and deaths were waiting for the Jewish people. (Jer. 16:1-4) I was persecuted and even threatened with death by the Jewish priests because of my condemnations to them.

When I was very old, I wrote a second book called Lamentations. I predicted Judah's downfall, but I did not lose my hope to return. I bought a field in my homeland just before I was taken off to exile. Who am I?

STEP 2 Speak!

오디오를 듣고 큰소리로 따라 읽어 보세요.

A 10-3

Isaiah: The Prophet Who Saw the Future

Isaiah means "Yahweh is my Salvation."[1]

He was known as one of the greatest prophets of Israel.

He proclaimed[2] God's coming judgements on Israel and upon the whole earth.

Especially, he criticized[3] the kings of Israel for their arrogance[4] and hypocrisy.[5]

Isaiah also told the Jewish people to repent[6] of their sins,[7] and have faith and follow the Lord even when His ways were not clear[8] to them.

He kept saying that God loved and cared for[9] them even though they did not deserve to[10] be loved by God.

He wrote many words about the coming Messiah, and because of this he was called the prophet who saw the future.

Words and Idioms Consult the index dictionary if needed.

1 **salvation**
the act of being saved by God from evil 구원

2 **proclaim**

3 **criticize**

4 **arrogance**

5 **hypocrisy**

6 **repent**

7 **sin**

8 **clear**

9 **care for**

10 **deserve to do**

B 10-4

Jeremiah: The Prophet Who Wept for the Israelites

Jeremiah was a prophet whose nickname[1] was "the weeping[2] prophet."
Jeremiah was consecrated[3] by God before he was born.
He had been called to preach since he was very young.
God forbade Jeremiah to[4] marry and have sons and daughters because only disasters[5] and deaths were waiting for the Jewish people. (Jer. 16:1-4)
Jeremiah was persecuted[6] and even threatened[7] with death by the Jewish priests because of his condemnations[8] to them.

When Jeremiah was very old, he wrote a second book called Lamentations.[9]
Jeremiah predicted Judah's downfall,[10] but he did not lose his hope to return.
This could be shown by his buying a field in his homeland just before he was taken off to exile.

Words and Idioms Consult the index dictionary if needed.

1 **nickname**

an informal name that your friends or family call you that is not your real name 별명

2 **weep**

3 **consecrate**

4 **forbid someone to do**

5 **disaster**

6 **persecute**

7 **threaten**

8 **condemnation**

9 **lamentation**

10 **downfall**

Grammar Points

수동형 문장 (Passive Sentences) ❷

이번 과에서는 앞서 미처 다 다루지 못한 수동형 문장에 대해 좀 더 알아보도록 하겠습니다.

❶ 〈by + 목적어〉가 생략되는 경우

수동형 문장에서 행위나 동작을 가한 사람이 분명하거나 굳이 밝힐 필요가 없을 때 〈by + 목적어〉를 생략할 수도 있습니다.

I **was born** in 1999. 난 1999년에 태어났다.

▶ 어머니에 의해 태어난 게 너무나 분명하므로 by my mom은 생략

That building **was built** in 2012.

▶ 누가 지었는지 굳이 밝힐 필요가 없는 경우

❷ by 대신 다른 전치사를 쓰는 경우

〈by + 목적어〉 자리에 by가 아니라 다른 전치사를 쓰는 경우도 있습니다.

Minju **is interested in** English literature. 민주는 영문학에 관심이 있다.

I'**m satisfied with** my job. 난 내 직업에 만족한다.

다른 전치사를 쓰는 수동형 동사 표현		
be disappointed in/with	be filled with	be interested in
be married to	be prepared for	be satisfied with
be scared of	be tired of	be worried about

Exercise 다음 우리말을 수동형 문장으로 영작해 보세요.

1 5000명이 넘는 사람이 태국에서 거대한 쓰나미로 죽었다.

힌트 great tsunami, kill, Thailand

2 그 그림은 아름다운 색으로 가득 차 있다.

힌트 be filled with

Let's Talk!

A Let's Memorize the Patterns. 10-5

deserve ~할 만한 자격이 있다

deserve는 참 좋은 단어입니다. 어떤 상이나 보상을 받을 때 그럴 만한 가치가 충분히 있다는 의미를 지닌 단어이죠. 본문에서처럼 〈deserve to + 동사원형〉의 형태로 쓸 수도 있고, 〈deserve + 명사〉로도 쓸 수 있습니다. 이 자리에서는 뒤에 명사가 오는 예문들을 몇 가지 연습해 보도록 하죠.

You **deserve** a rest after all that hard work. 그렇게 힘든 일을 했으니 쉴 만하네.

▶ 쉴 만한 자격이 있을 정도로 힘든 일을 했다는 의미입니다.

Minsu **deserves** the first prize. 민수는 일등상을 받을 만한 자격이 있어.

▶ 일등상을 받을 정도로 충분히 노력을 했다는 의미입니다.

B Let's Talk: Pair Work

두 명씩 짝을 지어 다음 대화를 나눠보세요. 그런 다음 Substitute Drills에 주어진 표현을 이용해 응용해 보세요.

1

Partner A I can't believe I won the first prize.

Partner B You **deserve** it. You studied very hard.

Substitute Drills

(1) Minjung - a scholarship (2) Sangmin - an honor prize

Confession & Prayer

A My Confession 10-6

Hundreds of years before Jesus was born, Isaiah wrote of His birth and works. “The virgin will be with child and will give birth to a son, and will call him Immanuel.” (Isaiah 7:14) “He will reign on David’s throne and over his kingdom, establishing and upholding it with justice and righteousness from that time on and forever. The zeal of the LORD Almighty will accomplish this.” (Isaiah 9:7) Isaiah even saw the sufferings and death of Jesus, the Messiah, but these sorrowful visions could not make him despair because God showed the redeeming power of Jesus’s death as well. Is it very amazing that the prophet who lived from approximately 740 to 700 B. C. foretold the story of Jesus, the Messiah? Share your idea with group members and write down your idea in English if you can.

예수가 태어나기 수백 년 전 이사야는 예수의 탄생과 하실 일에 대해 기록하였습니다. “처녀가 잉태하여 아들을 낳을 것이요 그의 이름을 임마누엘이라 하리라.”(이사야 7:14) “다윗의 왕좌와 그의 나라에 군림하여 그 나라를 굳게 세우고 그 이후로 영원히 정의와 공의로 그것을 보존하실 것이라. 만군의 여호와의 열심이 이를 이루시리라.”(이사야 9:7) 이사야는 메시아, 예수의 고통과 죽음까지도 보았습니다. 하지만 이런 애통한 비전으로 인해 이사야는 절망하지 않았습니다. 하나님께서 예수의 죽음의 대속적인 힘 역시 보여주셨기 때문입니다. 약 기원전 740년에서 700년까지 살았던 선지자가 메시아, 예수의 생애를 예언했다는 것이 놀랍지 않나요? 다른 친구들과 이야기를 나누어 본 후 여러분의 생각을 가능하면 영어로 써보세요.

* 대속: 예수가 십자가의 보혈(寶血)로 인류의 죄를 대신 씻어 구원한 일

영어로 쓰기가 힘들다면 우리말로 써도 괜찮습니다.

B Let's Pray! 10-7

예레미야가 왜 눈물의 선지자가 되었을까요? 이스라엘 사람들이 하나님에게 복종하려 하지 않았기 때문입니다. 예레미야는 사람들을 변화시키는 기도의 힘을 믿었습니다. 그래서 이스라엘 사람들을 위해 울면서 기도했습니다.

Ah, Sovereign LORD, you have made the heavens and the earth by your great power and outstretched arm. Nothing is too hard for you.

…

O great and powerful God, whose name is the LORD Almighty,

great are your purposes and mighty are your deeds. Your eyes are open to all the ways of men; you reward everyone according to his conduct and as his deeds deserve.

(Jeremiah 32:17 & 18b-19)

슬프도소이다 주 여호와여, 주께서 큰 능력과 펴신 팔로 천지를 지으셨사오니 주에게는 할 수 없는 일이 없으시니이다.

…

크고 능력 있으신 하나님이시요 이름은 만군의 여호와시니이다.

주는 책략에 크시며 하시는 일에 능하시며 인류의 모든 길을 주목하시며 그의 길과 그의 행위의 열매대로 보응하시나이다.

(예레미야 32:17 & 18b–19)

Write a Prayer for Yourself!

위의 기도문을 외워보세요. 다 외운 다음엔 직접 한번 써보세요.

Ah, Sovereign LORD,

Unto us a Child is Born

(to the tune 'Yankee Doodle')

Unto us a child is born,
to us a son is given,
and government around the world,
will be upon his shoulders.

Mighty God,
The Prince of Peace,
Everlasting Father.
Counsellor,
Most Wonderful.
His power will be endless.

And he will reign on David's throne,
and over all his kingdom.
Building and upholding it,
with righteousness and justice.

From that time for evermore,
His peace, it shall be endless.
His government shall never cease,
the Lord himself will do this.

Unto us a child is born,
to us a son is given,
and government around the world,
will be upon his shoulders.

Mighty God,
The Prince of Peace,
Everlasting Father.
Counsellor,
Most Wonderful.
His power will be endless.

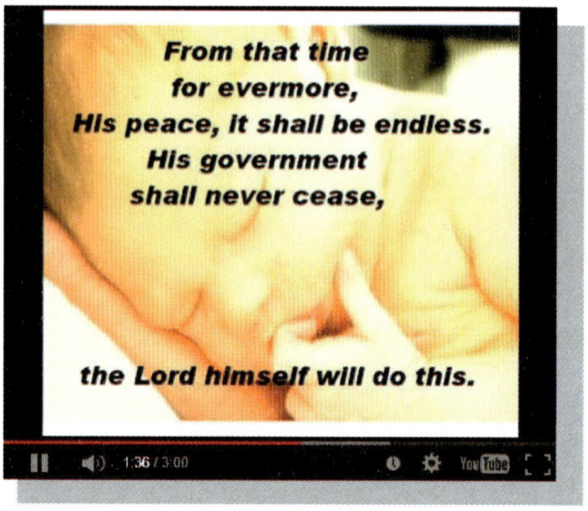

used with permission www.sheilahamil.co.uk

11

The Prophets during the Time of Babylon Captivity

I will bless them and the places surrounding my hill. I will send down showers in season; there will be showers of blessing. (Ezekiel 34:26)

Who Am I?

STEP 1 Listen!

오디오를 듣고 말하고 있는 인물이 누구인지 알아맞혀 보세요.

A

11-1

Who am I?

Script

A

I was a prophet and my name means "The Lord makes me strong." During the time of the Babylonian captivity, God called me to preach a message of hope.

One night I had a very strange dream. I walked with God in the middle of a large valley, which was filled with dry bones. God ordered me to say to these bones, "You will live. The Lord will breathe life into you and you will come to life. Then you will know that I am the Lord." I prophesied as I was commanded. Then, the bones came together, were covered with skin, and breath entered their bodies. They stood up on their feet, a vast army. Through this dream, God showed me the sign that the Israelites would live again like the dry bones in the valley. Who am I?

B

11-2

Who am I?

Script

B

I was a prophet and my name means "God is my judge." I was considered to be healthy, handsome and wise, so I was taken into King Nebuchadnezzar's court to be trained.

I became a court official because I interpreted King Nebuchadnezzar's dreams. Under King Belshazzar, the son of King Nebuchadnezzar, I also interpreted the handwriting on the wall.

King Darius loved me a lot, so I was envied by other court officials. Their cunning tactics led to me being thrown into a lions' den, but I survived because God's angel protected me through the night.

I saw some apocalyptic visions, so I wrote them in the book of the Bible with my name on it. Who am I?

STEP 2 Speak!

오디오를 듣고 큰소리로 따라 읽어 보세요.

A 11-3

Ezekiel: The Prophet Who Was Chosen as God's Watchman

Ezekiel was a prophet and his name means "The Lord makes me strong."
During the time of the Babylonian captivity,[1] God called Ezekiel to preach[2] a message of hope.

One night he had a very strange dream.
He walked with God in the middle of[3] a large valley,[4] which was filled with dry bones.[5]
God ordered him to say to these bones, "You will live.
The Lord will breathe life into you and you will come to life.[6]
Then you will know that I am the Lord."
Ezekiel prophesied[7] as he was commanded.[8]
Then, the bones came together, were covered with skin, and breath entered their bodies.
They stood up on their feet, a vast[9] army.
Through this dream, God showed him the sign[10] that the Israelites would live again like the dry bones in the valley.

Words and Idioms Consult the index dictionary if needed.

1 **captivity**

a situation in which a person is being kept as a prisoner 포로 신세, 감금 상태

2 **preach**

3 **in the middle of**

4 **valley**

5 **bone**

6 **come to life**

7 **prophesy**

8 **command**

9 **vast**

10 **sign**

B 11-4

Daniel: The Prophet Who Survived in the Lions' Den

Daniel was a prophet whose name means "God is my judge."
Daniel was considered to be healthy, handsome and wise, so he was taken into King Nebuchadnezzar's court[1] to be trained.

He became a court official[2] because he interpreted[3] King Nebuchadnezzar's dreams.
Under King Belshazzar, the son of King Nebuchadnezzar, Daniel also interpreted the handwriting[4] on the wall.

King Darius loved Daniel a lot, so other court officials envied him.
Their cunning[5] tactics[6] led to Daniel being thrown into a lions' den,[7] but he survived[8] because God's angel protected[9] him through the night.

Daniel saw some apocalyptic[10] visions, and he wrote these visions in the book of the Bible with his name on it.

Words and Idioms Consult the index dictionary if needed.

1 **court**
the place where a king or queen lives and works 궁정

2 **court official**

3 **interpret**

4 **handwriting**

5 **cunning**

6 **tactic**

7 **den**

8 **survive**

9 **protect**

10 **apocalyptic**

Grammar Points

현재분사(present participle)와 과거분사(past participle)

동사의 현재분사(동사원형+ing)와 과거분사(동사원형+ed)는 모두 형용사의 역할을 합니다. 이번 과에서는 이런 현재분사와 과거분사에 대해 살펴보도록 하죠.

❶ 명사를 수식하는 현재분사와 과거분사

현재분사와 과거분사는 뒤에 오는 명사를 수식할 수 있습니다. 이때 현재분사는 다음에 오는 명사의 입장에서 능동적인 의미를 지닐 때, 과거분사는 다음에 오는 명사의 입장에서 수동적인 의미를 지닐 때 사용됩니다.

It was an **exciting** game. 그것은 흥미진진한 경기였다.

Look at the **broken** window! 깨진 창문 좀 봐!

❷ be동사와 함께 하는 현재분사와 과거분사

이때 역시 현재분사는 주어의 능동적인 상태나 동작을 나타내고, 과거분사는 주어의 수동적인 상태나 동작을 나타내죠.

I'm **having** dinner. 난 저녁 먹고 있다.

▶ 〈be + -ing〉의 현재진행형 문장에서 -ing는 동사의 현재분사형. 이 문장에서 현재분사 having(먹고 있는)은 주어 I의 능동적인 동작을 나타냄

I'm **satisfied** with their service. 난 그들의 서비스에 만족한다.

▶ 〈be + p.p.〉의 수동형 문장에서 p.p.는 동사의 과거분사형. 이 문장에서 과거분사 satisfied(만족되어진)는 주어 I의 수동적인 상태를 나타냄

Exercise 주어진 동사를 다음 빈칸에 적절한 형태(현재분사나 과거분사)로 바꿔 써 보세요.

1 (surprise) I was ______________ by that news. It was ______________ news.

2 (interest) They are ______________ in that sound. It is an ______________ sound.

3 (amuse) Grandmother is telling them an ______________ story. They are ______________ children.

4 (confuse) The scientist got ______________ results. They are ______________ scientists.

5 (frighten) The strange noise frightened my family. It was a ______________ sound.

Let's Talk!

A Let's Memorize the Patterns. 11-5

stand up 일어서다

stand + 사람 + up ~를 바람맞히다

오늘은 stand up의 구어적(spoken) 의미를 알아보겠습니다. 아래 예문을 보세요. 첫 번째 문장에서 stand up은 '일어서다'의 의미입니다. 하지만 두 번째 문장은 '그가 나를 일으켜 세웠다.'는 뜻이 아닙니다. 또 뒤에 이어지는 문장으로 봐서는 말하는 사람이 화가 난 듯합니다. 여기서 〈stand + 사람 + up〉은 구어로 '~를 바람맞히다', 즉 약속시간에 나오지 않는 것을 말합니다.

They **stood up** on their feet, a vast army.
그들은 발을 딛고 일어서 거대한 군대가 되었다.

He **stood** me **up**! I will never talk to him again!
걔가 날 바람맞혔어! 다신 걔랑 말도 안 할 거야!

B Let's Talk: Pair Work

다음은 여자 또는 남자한테 바람맞았다고 얘기하는 친구에게 다신 그 여자 또는 그 남자한테 전화하지 말라고 하는 내용의 대화입니다. 두 명씩 짝을 지어 연습해 보세요.

1	Partner A	She/He **stood** me **up**!
	Partner B	Really? Don't ever call her/him again!
2	Partner A	I got **stood up**!
	Partner B	Really? Don't ever call her/him again!

She stood me up!과 I got stood up!
두 문장 모두 '바람맞았어'라는 같은 의미를 지니고 있습니다. 차이는 문장의 태(voice)로, She stood me up!은 능동형 문장이고, I got stood up!은 수동형 문장입니다. 의미상의 차이를 굳이 찾자면 수동형은 '나'를 중심으로 쓴 것이라는 점이죠. 두 문장 모두 매우 구어적인 표현으로 실생활에서 흔히 쓰이는 말이므로 잘 기억해뒀다 필요할 때 써보도록 하세요.

Confession & Prayer

A My Confession 11-6

Shadrach, Meshach, and Abednego were friends of Daniel. They were taken as prisoners to Babylon with Daniel. King Nebuchadnezzar made a huge golden statue and issued a decree that everyone must bow down and worship it. These three did not obey this. Because of this they were thrown into a fiery furnace. When the king looked into the furnace, there were four men walking around. One of them looked like an angel from God. The king saved their lives and made a new law that none should say anything bad about the God of these three men. If you were in their shoes, what would you do? Like Daniel's three friends, do you believe God will protect you? Share your idea with group members and write down your idea in English if you can.

사드락과 메삭과 아벳느고는 다니엘의 친구였습니다. 이들은 다니엘과 함께 바벨론에 포로로 잡혀갔습니다. 느부갓네살 왕은 거대한 금 신상을 만들어서 모든 사람이 엎드려 신상에 절을 해야 한다는 법령을 선포했죠. 이 세 친구들은 이 법령에 복종하지 않았고 이 때문에 이들은 맹렬히 타는 풀무불에 던져졌습니다. 그러나 풀무불을 본 왕은 네 사람이 걸어 다니는 것을 보았죠. 이들 중 한 사람은 하나님이 보내신 천사 같았습니다. 왕은 이들의 목숨을 구해주었고 어느 누구도 이 세 친구의 하나님에 대해 나쁘게 말해서는 안 된다는 새 법을 만들었습니다. 만약 여러분이 이 세 친구와 같은 상황에 처한다면 어떻게 하겠습니까? 다니엘의 세 친구처럼 하나님께서 여러분을 보호해 주신다는 것을 믿나요? 다른 친구들과 이야기를 나누어 본 후 여러분의 생각을 가능하면 영어로 써보세요.

영어로 쓰기가 힘들다면 우리말로 써도 괜찮습니다.

B Let's Pray! 11-7

하나님이 예루살렘의 황폐함을 끝내기로 선지자들에게 약속하신 70년이 다가오자 다니엘은 베옷을 입고 금식하며 하나님께 기도하였습니다. 다니엘서 9장 4절에서 19절은 기도로 이루어진 구절입니다. 간단하게 다음의 구절을 볼까요?

O Lord, the great and awesome God,
who keeps his covenant of love with all who love him
and obey his commands,
we have sinned and done wrong.
We have been wicked and have rebelled;
we have turned away from your commands and laws.
…
The Lord our God is merciful and forgiving,
even though we have rebelled against him.

(Daniel 9:4-5 & 9)

크시고 두려워할 주 하나님,
주를 사랑하고 주의 계명을 지키는 자를 위하여 언약을 지키시고 그에게 인자를 베푸시는 이시여,
우리는 이미 범죄하여 패역하며
행악하며 반역하여
주의 법도와 규례를 떠났사오며
…
주 우리 하나님께는 긍휼과 용서하심이 있사오니
이는 우리가 주께 패역하였음이오며

(다니엘 9:4-5 & 9)

Write a Prayer for Yourself!

위의 기도문을 외운 다음 직접 한번 써보세요. 그런 다음, 다니엘서 9장 4절에서 19절까지의 기도 전문도 한번 읽어보세요.

O Lord,

A Poem & Song

Daniel was a Man of Prayer

(to the tune 'London Bridge is Falling Down')

Daniel was a man of prayer.
He prayed here, he prayed there;
prayed about just anywhere,
despite those who opposed him.

Darius was the king back then,
appointed many serving men.
He promoted one of them;
he admired Daniel.

Jealous servants told the king,
all should worship only him.
They knew this law would be a sin
for poor Daniel.

The wicked servants got their way,
just like hawks, watched each day.
Arrested Daniel straight away
when they caught him praying.

The law could not be changed by then,
so these scheming gentlemen,
threw him in a lions' den.
This is what they wanted.

The king was sad, that he'd agreed
Daniel should be lion feed!
So next morning ran with speed,
to see if he was living.

"An angel sealed the lions' jaws!"
cried Daniel, "King, I'm truly yours!"
So into the den instead,
went those who had opposed him.

used with permission www.sheilahamil.co.uk

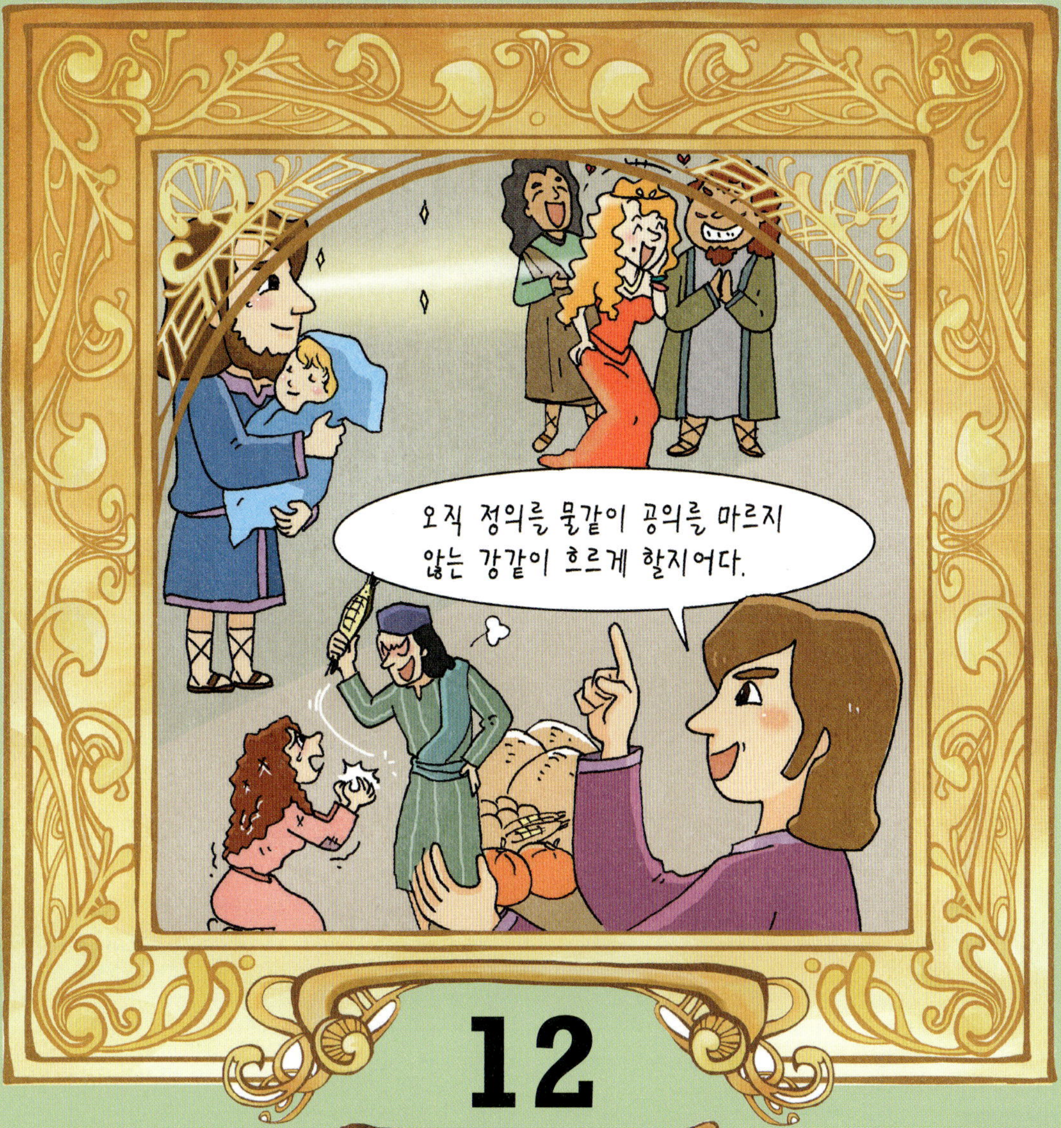

12

The Prophets Who Shouted 'Justice'

Seek good, not evil, that you may live. Then the LORD God Almighty will be with you, just as you say he is. (Amos 5:14)

Who Am I?

STEP 1 Listen!

오디오를 듣고 말하고 있는 인물이 누구인지 알아맞혀 보세요.

A

12-1

Who am I?

Script

A

I was a prophet. I was from the Northern Kingdom. To the Israelites, I preached stop sinning and change their ways because committing sins meant separation from God. I also gave them a strong warning that the blessing of God would soon be gone if they did not stop sinning. I kept preaching to them that God would give forgiveness to those who truly repented and asked for forgiveness, but they would not listen. They did not know they would be conquered by the armies of Assyria. It was pitiful to see that the Israelites behaved like the woman who ran away from her generous husband. My marriage to Gomer was a symbol of God's relationship to Israel. Who am I?

B

12-2

Who am I?

Script

B

I was a simple shepherd from Tekoa in the Southern Kingdom. I only knew how to care for my sheep. But one day God gave me a powerful message to deliver to the Israelites. I started to preach against Israel's neighbours and how they were unjust. I also saw that the prosperous Israelites ignored the poor and the needy, so I shouted the repentance of their sins and God's punishment to them. When the Israelites started to pay attention to my preaching, I pronounced Israel's destruction. But my messages included a promise from God as well. My famous message was "Let justice roll on like a river, righteousness like a never-failing stream!" (Amos 5:24) Who am I?

STEP 2 Speak!

오디오를 듣고 큰소리로 따라 읽어 보세요.

A 12-3

Hosea: The Prophet Who Was Mentioned First among Twelve Minor Prophets

Hosea was a prophet.

He was from the Northern Kingdom.

To the Israelites, Hosea preached stop sinning and change their ways because committing sins[1] meant separation[2] from God.

He also gave them a strong warning[3] that the blessing of God would soon be gone if they did not stop sinning.

He kept preaching to them that God would give forgiveness to those who truly repented[4] and asked for forgiveness, but they would not listen.

They did not know they would be conquered[5] by the armies of Assyria.

It was pitiful[6] for Hosea to see that the Israelites behaved[7] like the woman who ran away from[8] her generous[9] husband.

Hosea's marriage to Gomer was a symbol of God's relationship[10] to Israel.

Words and Idioms Consult the index dictionary if needed.

1 **commit a sin**

to do an action, thought, or way of behaving that is wrong according to religious laws 죄를 짓다

2 **separation**

3 **warning**

4 **repent**

5 **conquer**

6 **pitiful**

7 **behave**

8 **run away from**

9 **generous**

10 **relationship**

B 12-4

Amos: The Prophet Who Was a Shepherd

Amos was a simple shepherd from Tekoa in the Southern Kingdom.

One day, God gave him a powerful message to deliver[1] to the Israelites.

So Amos was sent to the Northern Kingdom and started to preach against Israel's neighbours and how they were unjust.[2]

Amos saw the contrast[3] between how the rich[4] and the poor[5] lived.

He also saw how the prosperous[6] Israelites ignored[7] the poor and the needy.[8]

When the Israelites started to listen to his preaching, he pronounced[9] Israel's destruction.[10]

Nevertheless, his messages included a promise from God as well.

His famous message was "Let justice roll on like a river, righteousness like a never-failing stream!" (Amos 5:24)

Words and Idioms Consult the index dictionary if needed.

1 **deliver**

to give a formal talk to a group of people 전하다

2 **unjust**

3 **contrast**

4 **the rich**

5 **the poor**

6 **prosperous**

7 **ignore**

8 **the needy**

9 **pronounce**

10 **destruction**

Grammar Points

접속사 and, but, or, so

이번 과에서는 접속사 and(그리고, ~와/과), but(그러나, 하지만), or(또는, 아니면), so(그래서)에 대해서 살펴보도록 하죠.

접속사 and, but, or는 등위접속사라 불립니다. 등위접속사는 저울처럼 두 개, 혹은 그 이상의 것들의 무게가 같음을 의미합니다. 해석은 앞에서부터 하며, 이 등위접속사가 연결하는 것들은 품사나 형태가 같아야 합니다. so는 결과를 나타내는 접속사로 그 앞에 항상 쉼표(,)를 씁니다.

I always put milk **and** sugar in my coffee. 난 커피에 항상 우유와 설탕을 넣는다.
(milk: 명사, sugar: 명사)

I went to the movie with my mom, dad, **and** younger sister. 엄마, 아빠, 그리고 여동생과 함께 영화를 보러 갔다.
(my mom: 명사 (쉼표), dad: 명사 (쉼표), younger sister: 명사)

Heesun is probably doing her laundry **or** watching TV. 희선이는 아마도 빨래를 하고 있거나 TV를 보고 있는 것 같다.
(doing her laundry: 동사의 현재진행형, watching TV: 동사의 현재진행형)

I cleaned my room, **but** it is still untidy. 방을 청소했지만, 아직도 지저분하다.
(I cleaned my room: 절, it is still untidy: 절)

I needed some T-shirts, **so** I went shopping. 티셔츠가 필요해서 쇼핑하러 갔다.
(I needed some T-shirts: 절 (쉼표), I went shopping: 절)

Exercise 다음 우리말을 보고 빈칸에 알맞은 접속사를 넣어보세요.

1 그 남자는 개를 산책시키거나 축구를 하고 있다.
He is walking the dog ________ playing soccer.

2 엄마와 아빠는 지금 집에 계신다.
Mom ________ Dad are home now.

3 영어는 어렵지만 재미있다.
English is hard ________ fun.

4 주스, 코카콜라, 아니면 물 중에 어느 걸로 마실래?
Which one do you want, juice, coke, ________ water?

5 희진이는 피곤해서 집에 갔다.
Heejin was tired, ________ she went home.

Let's Talk!

A Let's Memorize the Patterns. 12-5

stop to + 동사원형 ~하기 위해서 멈추다

stop + -ing ~하는 것을 멈추다

'멈추다'의 의미를 지닌 동사 stop은 그 다음에 〈to + 동사원형〉이 오느냐, 아니면 -ing가 오느냐에 따라 그 뜻이 달라집니다. 주의하세요!

Hosea preached **stop sinning** to the Israelites.
호세아는 이스라엘 백성들에게 죄 짓는 것을 멈추라고 설교했다.

They **stop to read** the sign.
그 사람들은 표지판을 읽기 위해 멈췄다.

B Let's Talk: Pair Work

두 명씩 짝을 지어 다음 대화를 나눠보세요.

1

Partner A **Stop beating** around the bushes! What is the bottom line?

Partner B Well. All I'm saying is that I want you to lend me some money.

Stop beating around the bushes. 말 그만 빙빙 돌려라. | What is the bottom line? 하고 싶은 말이 뭐냐? | All I'm saying is that S + V 내가 하고자 하는 말은 ~이다 | I want you to + 동사원형 네가 ~해주면 좋겠다, ~해줬으면 한다

2

Partner A **Stop beating** around the bushes! What is your point?

Partner B Well, All I'm saying is that I want you ______________ .

What is your point? 하고 싶은 말이 뭐냐?

Confession & Prayer

A My Confession 12-6

As a prophet, Amos saw that the Israelites did not follow God's words and commandments even though they were enjoying great wealth. Amos delivered a strong message that God might send them unpleasant things into their lives in order to keep them from sinning. He also preached that they should obey God in order to be His friends. Despite Amos's strong messages, the Israelites would not listen. They did not care about the poor and needy. They did not stop sinning against God's Words. Like the Israelites in the time of Amos, have you forgotten to give thanks to God when everything goes well? Share your idea with group members and write down your idea in English if you can.

선지자로서 아모스는 이스라엘 백성들이 잘 살면서도 여호와 하나님의 말씀과 명령을 따르지 않음을 보았습니다. 아모스는 여호와 하나님이 그들의 삶에 좋지 않은 것들을 보내 더 이상 죄를 짓지 않도록 할 수도 있다는 강력한 메시지를 전했습니다. 아모스는 또한 하나님의 친구가 되기 위해서 하나님에게 복종해야만 한다고 설교했습니다. 아모스의 이런 강한 메시지에도 불구하고 이스라엘 백성들은 들으려 하지 않았습니다. 이들은 가난하고 궁핍한 사람들을 경시했습니다. 여호와 하나님의 말씀에 반하여 죄를 짓는 것을 멈추지 않았습니다. 아모스 시대의 이스라엘 백성들처럼 모든 일이 잘될 때 하나님께 감사드리는 걸 잊은 경험이 있나요? 다른 친구들과 이야기를 나누어 본 후 여러분의 생각을 가능하면 영어로 써보세요.

영어로 쓰기가 힘들다면 우리말로 써도 괜찮습니다.

B Let's Pray! 12-7

다음은 시편 1장 1절에서 3절까지의 구절입니다. 진심을 담아 천천히 소리 내어 읽은 다음, 가능하면 외워보세요.

Blessed is the man
who does not walk in the counsel of the wicked
or stand in the way of sinners
or sit in the seat of mockers.
But his delight is in the law of the LORD,
and on his law he meditates day and night.
He is like a tree planted by streams of water,
which yields its fruit in season
and whose leaf does not wither.
Whatever he does prospers.

(Psalms 1:1-3)

복 있는 사람들은
악인들의 꾀를 따르지 아니하며
죄인들의 길에 서지 아니하며
오만한 자들의 자리에 앉지 아니하고
오직 여호와의 율법을 즐거워하여
그의 율법을 주야로 묵상하는도다.
그는 시냇가에 심은 나무가
철을 따라 열매를 맺으며
그 잎사귀가 마르지 아니함 같으니
그가 하는 모든 일이 다 형통하리로다.

(시편 1:1–3)

Write a Prayer for Yourself!

위의 시편 내용을 다 외웠나요? 다 외운 다음엔 직접 한번 써보세요.

A Poem & Song

Song of Amos

I will tell you a brand new story,
I will sing an ancient song,
for this people turn against me,
do not know their right from wrong.

I despise empty worship,
cannot stand vain offerings.
Can't abide the gifts they bring me,
close my ears to songs they sing.

But let justice roll on freely,
like a river running clean.
Righteousness be found among you,
like a never failing stream.

Look at all their endless idols!
They have turned their backs on me.
All secure and so complacent,
look with eyes that cannot see.

They are bound with cords of darkness,
held in bonds of misery.
Turn to me my captive people,
I your God can set you free.

But let justice roll on freely,
like a river running clean.
Righteousness be found among you,
like a never failing stream.

But let justice roll on freely,
like a river running clean.
Righteousness be found among you,
like a never failing stream.

like a never failing stream
like a never failing stream
like a never failing stream
like a never failing stream...

used with permission www.sheilahamil.co.uk

13

The Prophet Who Was Swallowed by a Large Fish

When my life was ebbing away, I remembered you, LORD, and my prayer rose to you, to your holy temple. (Jonah 2:7)

Who Am I?

STEP 1 Listen!

오디오를 듣고 말하고 있는 인물이 누구인지 알아맞혀 보세요.

A

13-1

Who am I?

Script

A

I was a prophet, and my name means 'dove.' God called me to go to Nineveh and preach repentance to the people of it, but I took a ship to Tarshish in order to get away from God. The ship met a great storm and the sailors cast lots to see who angered God. I was chosen and thrown into the sea. I was swallowed by a large fish and lived in its belly for three days and nights. I gave thanks to God and prayed that I would obey God's words. Immediately the fish went to dry land and spit me out.

I went to Nineveh and proclaimed, "Forty more days and Nineveh will be overturned." (Jonah 3:4) Everybody in Nineveh believed my words and turned from their evil ways. Who am I?

B

13-2

Who am I?

Script

B

I was a prophet and my name means 'my messenger.' The book of the Bible with my name on it is the last one of the Old Testament even though I lived in Jerusalem just before the return of Ezra and Nehemiah along with the exiles.

As a prophet, I denounced priests' disrespect for worship practices and the failure to pay tithes. I also pointed out the unfaithfulness and injustice of the Israelites. I also preached to repent and live righteously. One of my important messages is "But for you who revere my name, the sun of righteousness will rise with healing in its wings. And you will go out and leap like calves released from the stall." (Malachi 4:2) Who am I?

STEP 2 Speak!

오디오를 듣고 큰소리로 따라 읽어 보세요.

A 13-3

Jonah: The Prophet Who Was Swallowed by a Large Fish

Jonah was a prophet, and his name means 'dove.'[1]

God called Jonah to go to Nineveh and preach repentance[2] to its people, but Jonah took a ship to Tarshish in order to get away from[3] God.

The ship met a great storm and the sailors cast lots[4] to see who angered God.

Jonah was chosen and thrown into the sea.

He was swallowed[5] by a large fish and lived in its belly[6] for three days and nights.

Jonah gave thanks to God and prayed that he would obey[7] God's words.

Immediately the fish went to dry land and spit him out.[8]

He went to Nineveh and proclaimed,[9] "Forty more days and Niveveh will be overturned."[10] (Jonah 3:4)

Everybody in Nineveh believed his words and turned from their evil ways.

Words and Idioms Consult the index dictionary if needed.

1 **dove**

a white bird often used as a sign meaning peace 비둘기

2 **repentance**

3 **get away from**

4 **cast lots**

5 **swallow**

6 **belly**

7 **obey**

8 **spit out**

9 **proclaim**

10 **overturn**

B 13-4

Malachi: The Prophet Whose Book Was Written Last in the Old Testament

Malachi was a prophet and his name means 'my messenger.'

The book of the Bible with his name on it is the last one of the Old Testament even though he lived in Jerusalem just before the return of Ezra and Nehemiah along with the exiles.[1]

As a prophet, Malachi denounced[2] priests' disrespect for worship practices[3] and the failure to pay tithes.[4]

He also pointed out[5] the unfaithfulness and injustice[6] of the Israelites.

To them, he always preached to repent and live righteously.

One of his important messages is "But for you who revere[7] my name, the sun of righteousness will rise with healing[8] in its wings.

And you will go out and leap[9] like calves released from the stall."[10] (Malachi 4:2)

Words and Idioms Consult the index dictionary if needed.

1 **exile**

someone who has been forced to live in a foreign country because they cannot live in their own country, usually for political reasons 유배자

2 **denounce**

3 **worship practice**

4 **tithe**

5 **point out**

6 **injustice**

7 **revere**

8 **heal**

9 **leap**

10 **stall**

Grammar Points

접속사 because, even though

이번 과에서는 이유를 나타내는 접속사 because(~ 때문에)와 반전을 나타내는 접속사 even though (~인데도 불구하고)에 대해서 살펴보도록 하겠습니다.

because와 even though는 모두 주절(main clause)을 필요로 하는 종속접속사입니다. because나 even though가 이끄는 종속절이 주절보다 앞에 올 때에 종속절이 끝나는 부분에 쉼표를 찍습니다. 그러나 이 순서가 바뀔 때에는 쉼표를 쓰지 않습니다.

Even though I wasn't prepared, I had to take that exam.

종속절 / 주절

= I had to take that exam **even though** I wasn't prepared.

준비가 되지 않았지만 난 그 시험을 쳐야만 했다.

Because she wasn't prepared, she postponed the presentation for another day.

종속절 / 주절

= She postponed the presentation for another day **because** she wasn't prepared.

그 여자는 준비가 되지 않았기 때문에 다른 날로 발표를 연기했다.

Exercise 다음 우리말을 영어로 써보세요.

1 수진이는 아팠기 때문에 학교에 결석했다.

Because ______________________________

= Sujin ______________________________

힌트 sick, absent from school

2 우리는 점심을 많이 먹었지만 푸드 코트에서 간식을 샀다.

Even though ______________________________

= We ______________________________

힌트 a big lunch, snacks

Let's Talk!

A Let's Memorize the Patterns. 13-5

spare a. 여분의 n. (예비 열쇠, 예비 타이어와 같은) 예비품
v. (돈, 시간을) 할애하다, (나쁜 일을) 면하게 하다

다음 코너인 〈My Confession〉에서 여호와 하나님께서 니느웨 성읍을 파멸하지 않고 '살려두다'라고 표현할 때 spare란 단어를 씁니다. spare란 단어는 알아두면 많은 도움이 되는 단어이므로 이 자리에서 익혀두도록 합니다.

I have a flat tire and no **spare**.
펑크가 났는데 예비 타이어가 없네.

A: Are you free today? 오늘 시간이 있니?
B: I don't have any time to **spare** today. 오늘은 짬을 낼 시간이 없어.

B Let's Talk: Pair Work

두 명씩 짝을 지어 다음 대화를 나눠보세요.

1

Partner A Are you free today?

Partner B 시간 없어. / 시간 많아.

시간이 없을 경우	시간이 있을 경우
I don't have any time to **spare** today. Not a moment to **spare**. I have no time to **spare**.	I have a lot of time to **spare**.

Confession & Prayer

A My Confession 13-6

Jonah has been considered as a reluctant prophet because he tried to run away from God when God called him to go to Nineveh. He did not like Nineveh, so he did not want God to save that city. After he returned to Nineveh and saw that God changed His mind and spared it, he got angry and said to God he would rather die than live. He also said to God he would rather die than live when God appointed a worm to attack the vine that gave him shade during the day. Have you turned away from God or complained to God when God asks you to do the things that you do not want? Share your idea with group members and write down your idea in English if you can.

요나는 여호와 하나님께서 니느웨로 가라고 부르실 때 도망가려 했기 때문에 주저하는 선지자로 간주됩니다. 요나는 니느웨를 좋아하지 않아서 여호와 하나님께서 그 성읍을 구하는 것을 원하지 않았습니다. 니느웨로 돌아가 하나님께서 마음을 바꿔 니느웨를 파멸시키지 않은 것을 목격한 요나는 화가 나서 하나님께 자신은 사는 것보다 죽는 것이 낫겠다고 말했습니다. 그는 또한 낮에 자신에게 그늘을 주었던 박넝쿨을 하나님께서 벌레를 주어 시들게 하시는 것을 보고 살기보다는 죽는 게 낫다고 말했습니다. 하나님께서 여러분이 하기를 원하지 않는 일을 시키실 때 외면을 하거나 불평을 한 적이 있습니까? 다른 친구들과 이야기를 나누어 본 후 여러분의 생각을 가능하면 영어로 써보세요.

영어로 쓰기가 힘들다면 우리말로 써도 괜찮습니다.

B Let's Pray! 13-7

요나는 니느웨로 가라는 하나님의 말씀을 듣지 않고 배를 타고 다른 곳으로 갔습니다. 폭풍우를 만난 선원들이 요나를 물속에 던져버리자, 큰 물고기(고래로 생각됨)가 요나를 삼켰습니다. 고래의 뱃속에서 요나는 다음과 같이 여호와 하나님께 기도드렸습니다. 요나의 마음을 생각하며 큰 소리로 읽어보세요.

In my distress I called to the LORD,
and he answered me.
From the depth of the grave I called for help,
and you listened to my cry.
…
While my life was ebbing away,
I remembered you, LORD,
and my prayer rose to you, to your holy temple.

(Jonah 2:2 & 7)

내가 받는 고난으로 말미암아 여호와께 불러 아뢰었더니
주께서 내게 대답하셨고
내가 스올의 뱃속에서 부르짖었더니
주께서 내 음성을 들으셨나이다.
…
내 영혼이 내 속에서 피곤할 때에
내가 여호와를 생각하였더니
내 기도가 주께 이르렀사오며 주의 성전에 미쳤나이다.

* 스올: 밑바닥이 없는 깊은 곳 (요나 2:2 & 7)

Write a Prayer for Yourself!

위의 기도문을 외운 다음 직접 한번 써보세요. 그런 다음, 성경책을 펼쳐 요나 2장의 기도문도 전부 한번 읽어보세요.

A Poem & Song

Go Jonah

(to the tune 'Six Little Ducks')

God spoke to Jonah, and he said , "Up!
Go down to Nineveh, they're corrupt!"
But Jonah had a 'mind block' with the word 'obey'
didn't want to go, and so he ran away, he ran away.

Off he sailed, to Tarshish in a boat.
Wibble wobble, wibble wobble, would it stay afloat?
Then an angry storm broke out upon the sea,
which put all those aboard in jeo-par-dy, in jeopardy.

The sailors said, "Oh let us all draw lots,
see who's responsible, the boat's awash!"
So they all drew lots, and put it to the test.
The lot fell to Jonah, and he confessed, he confessed.

Over the side did Jonah go.
Wibble wobble, wibble wobble, down below.
Then a whale came by and swallowed him whole.
Poor old Jonah, poor-old-soul, poor old soul!

He was there three nights, three days,
so he prayed to mend his ways.
So when the whale spat him upon the shore,
off to Nineveh he did go, he did go.

So he preached to the people there,
they wibble wobbled, full of trouble, everywhere.
But they did repent and Jonah took the huff;
left the city he had had enough, had enough.

A castor-oil plant grew over him,
protected him when he felt grim.
But it withered away which made poor Jonah mad,
God feels the same, when we are bad, when we are bad.

used with permission www.sheilahamil.co.uk

Activity

Let's Enjoy Speed Game!

다음은 우리가 지금까지 공부했던 구약의 인물 카드입니다. 두 명씩 팀을 이루어 주어진 시간 안에 한 사람은 영어로 인물을 설명하고, 다른 한 사람은 그 설명을 듣고 인물의 이름을 맞혀보세요.

- 제한 시간은 임의로 결정하면 됩니다.
- 인물 카드는 절취선을 따라 하나씩 분리한 다음, 섞어서 사용하세요.
- 게임을 시작하기 전에 지금까지 공부한 내용을 다시 한 번 죽 훑어보며 인물의 특징을 다시금 정리해 보도록 합니다.

Saul

Jonathan

David

Goliath

Solomon

Joash

Josiah

Elijah

Jezebel

Elisha

Naaman

Ezra

Nehemiah

Esther

Mordecai

Job

Isaiah

Jeremiah

Ezekiel

Daniel

Hosea

Amos

Jonah

Malachi

ANSWERS

for Grammar Points

01 • The First King of Israel

Grammar Points > Exercise

1 am meeting **2** am going / are, going **3** am taking

02 • The Man after God's Own Heart

Grammar Points > Exercise

1 stops **2** see **3** go **4** call **5** take

▶ 1번처럼 주어가 3인칭 단수인 경우엔 현재 시제로 동사 뒤에 -s를 붙여줘야 합니다.

03 • The King of Great Wisdom

Grammar Points > Exercise

1 thinks **2** have **3** is thinking **4** Do, need

04 • Two Kings Who Repaired God's House

Grammar Points > Exercise

1 My family have been to Gyeongju.

2 Have you seen that movie?

3 I have seen him before.

05 • The Man Who Was Fed by Ravens

Grammar Points > Exercise

1 We have just eaten lunch.
We just ate lunch.

2 Mom has already hung up the phone.
Mom already hung up the phone.

06 • The Bald Prophet

Grammar Points > Exercise

1 I have lived here since I was a child.

2 I have had this bike for three years.

3 My younger brother has studied Chinese since last year.

07 • The Teacher Well Versed in the Law of Moses

Grammar Points > Exercise

1 looked for / had left

2 was not / had just went out

3 met / had not seen

09 • Very Rich Man Who Lived in the Land of Uz

Grammar Points > Exercise

1 This sweater was made by my mom.

2 The Eiffel tower was designed by Alexander Eiffel.

3 수동형으로 바꿀 수 없음

10 • The Prophet Who Saw the Future

Grammar Points > Exercise

1 More than 5,000 people were killed by the great tsunami in Thailand.

2 That picture is filled with beautiful colors.

11 • The Prophets during the Time of Babylon Captivity

Grammar Points > Exercise

1 surprised / surprising
2 interested / interesting
3 amusing / amused
4 confusing / confused
5 frightening

▶ 첫 번째 문장의 frightened는 과거분사가 아니라 문장의 동사로, 과거 시제를 나타내고 있습니다.

12 • The Prophets Who Shouted 'Justice'

Grammar Points > Exercise

1 or 2 and 3 but 4 or 5 so

13 • The Prophet Who Was Swallowed by a Large Fish

Grammar Points > Exercise

1 Because Sujin was sick, she was absent from school.
Sujin was absent from school because she was sick.

2 Even though we had had a big lunch, we bought snacks at the food court.
We bought snacks at the food court even though we had had a big lunch.

Index Dictionary

for Words and Idioms

A

a piece of cake: something that is very easy 식은 죽 먹기

accept: to agree to do what someone asks 부탁을 받아들이다

according to: as stated by someone ~의 말에 따라서

all one's life: from someone's birth until their death 한평생

altar: a special table where religious ceremonies are performed, especially in a Christian church 제단

anoint: to put oil on a part of someone's body in a religious ceremony 기름을 부어 신성하게 하다

apocalyptic: describing or expecting a time when very bad things will happen or the world will be destroyed 종말론적인

appoint: to choose someone to do a particular job or have a particular position 임명하다

armor: metal clothing that soldiers wore in the Middle Ages to protect their bodies 갑옷

arrogance: behaviour that shows that you think you are better or more important than other people 오만

as well: in addition to something or someone else ~도 또한

as well as something/somebody: in addition to something or someone else ~뿐 아니라

ask: to speak or write to someone in order to get information from them 묻다

ask someone for forgiveness: to speak or write to someone because you want them to forgive 용서를 구하다

ask someone to do: to expect someone to do something or give you something ~에게 …해달라고 부탁[요청]하다

assemble: to come together and form a group 모이다

B

bald: with little or no hair on your head 대머리인

beg someone to do: to ask for help, an opportunity etc in a way that shows you want it very much ~에게 …을 해달라고 간청하다

behave: to do things in a particular way 처신하다

belly: a stomach 배

blame: to say or think that someone or something is responsible for an accident, problem, or bad situation 비난하다

bone: one of the hard parts that form a frame inside the body of a human or animal 뼈

bow down to someone: to show respect to someone who is more powerful than you ~에게 절하다, 예를 표하다

brave: capable of dealing with danger or pain, without seeming to be frightened 용감한

bring ~ together: to create a situation in which people meet and do something together, especially when they would not usually do so ~를 화해시키다

by virtue of: because of ~때문에

C

call on: to officially ask a person or organization to do something 요청하다

capable: very good at doing a job 유능한

captivity: a situation in which a person is being kept as a prisoner 포로 신세, 감금 상태

care for: to love someone 좋아하다

cast lots: decide who is going to do something by using a method in which each person takes a piece of paper or a stick and the person who has the paper with a special mark on or the shortest stick is chosen 제비뽑기를 하다

chariot: a vehicle with two wheels and no roof that was pulled by horses in races and battles in ancient times 전차

check: to examine someone or something 살펴보다

cheer: to shout in praise, approval, or support 응원하다, 성원하다

clear: obvious and impossible to doubt 분명한

come to life: to start to be alive 소생하다

command: to officially order someone to do something 명령하다

commander: one in an official position of command or control 지휘자

commandment: according to the Bible, one of the ten rules of behaviour called the Ten Commandments that God gave people to obey 계명

commit a sin: to do an action, thought, or way of behaving that is wrong according to religious laws 죄를 짓다

condemnation: a public statement in which someone criticizes someone or something severely 비난

conquer: to take control of land or people using soldiers 정복하다

consecrate: to perform a religious ceremony in order to make someone a priest, bishop, king, or queen 신성하게 하다, 성화하다

contrary to: completely different or opposed to something else ~과는 정반대로

contrast: a noticeable difference between people or things 대비

convince: to persuade someone to do something 설득하다

court: the place where a king or queen lives and works 궁정

court official: someone with an important position in the place where a king or queen lives and works 궁정 관리

covenant: a formal agreement or promise 약속, 계약

criticize: to say what you think is wrong or bad about something 비판하다

cunning: clever and good at deceiving people 교활한

cupbearer: someone who carries a drinking cup for a king 술 관원

cure: to stop someone from being affected by an illness 치료하다

curse: to say or think offensive or impolite words about someone or something 저주하다

cut: to use a knife, pair of scissors, or other sharp tool to divide something into two or more pieces 자르다

D

damage: to harm something physically so that it is broken, spoiled, or injured 손상시키다, 훼손하다

debt: an amount of money that you owe 빚

dedicate: to give to a holy purpose, often with a solemn ceremony 봉헌하다

defend: to say things to support someone or something that is being criticized 변호하다

deliver: to give a formal talk to a group of people 전하다

den: the home of some wild animals 굴, 우리

denounce: to criticize someone or something severely in public 맹렬히 비난하다

deprive: to take something away from someone 빼앗다

descendant: a relative of a person who lived in the past 후손

deserve to do: to have earned something by good actions ~할 만한 자격이 있다

desire: a strong feeling of wanting to have or to do something 욕구

destruction: damage that is so severe that something stops existing or can never return to its normal state 멸망

devise: to invent a method of doing something 고안하다, 꾸며내다

dew: small drops of water that form on the ground during the night 이슬

difference: something that makes one thing or person not the same as another thing or person 차이

dip: to lower something into a liquid for a moment before taking it back out again 담그다

disaster: something very bad that happens and causes a lot of damage or kills a lot of people 재난

disobey: to refuse to do what someone with authority tells you to do, or refuse to obey a rule or law 복종하지 않다

dove: a white bird often used as a sign meaning peace 비둘기

downfall: a sudden loss of power, status, or success 몰락

drive: to make someone determined to do something 몰아붙이다

E

earthly: relating to life on earth rather than to heaven 지상에 사는

encourage someone to do: to suggest that someone does something that you believe would be good ~에게 …을 하라고 격려하다

entire: all or every part of something 모든

escape: to get away from a place or dangerous situation when someone is trying to catch you or stop you 도망가다

exile: ❶ a situation in which you are forced to live in a foreign country 망명, 추방 ❷ someone who has been forced to live in a foreign country because they cannot live in their own country, usually for political reasons 유배자

F

faith: belief in a god or gods 믿음

faithful: continuing to do or believe something, even in a difficult situation 신실한

fall down: to move quickly downwards from a higher position 떨어지다

fiery: burning or full of flames 불타는

fix: to repair something 고치다, 수리하다

flesh: a person's skin 피부

forbid someone from doing: to tell someone that they must not do something ~에게 …하지 말라고 하다

forbid someone to do: to tell someone that they must not do something ~에게 …하지 말라고 하다

forever: for all time in the future 영원히

forgive: to decide that you will not be angry with someone who has offended, upset, or harmed you 용서하다

furious: extremely angry 몹시 화가 난

G

generous: tending to see the good qualities in someone 너그러운, 관대한

get away from: to escape from a person or place 도망치다

give ~ over to someone: if you give something over to someone, it becomes theirs ~을 …에게 주다, 양도하다

give back: to give someone something that they owned or had before 돌려주다

governor: an official who is sent by the central government to govern an area of the country 총독

H

handwriting: written words by hand 손으로 쓴 글씨

hang: to kill someone by putting a rope around their neck and making them fall 교수형에 처하다

happen to do: to do something by chance 우연히 ~하다

heal: ❶ to get better after an illness 치유되다 ❷ to make a part of the body healthy again after an injury 낫게 하다

hide: to put something in a place so that no one can find or see it 숨기다

hypocrisy: behaviour in which someone claims to have certain moral principles or beliefs but behaves in a way that shows they are not sincere 위선

I

idol: picture or statue that is worshipped as a god 우상

ignore: to not consider something, or to not let it influence you 무시하다

in the middle of: in the center of ~의 가운데에

include: to make someone or something part of a group, set, or collection of things 포함하다, 수록하다

injustice: an unfair action or event 불평등, 불의

insist: to keep saying very firmly that something is true, even when other people will not believe you 주장하다

intent on: determined to do something ~하기로 결의한

interpret: to explain the meaning of something 해석하다

invite someone to: to formally ask someone to go somewhere ~를 …로 초대하다

J

jealous of: feeling angry and unhappy because someone has something that you wish you had ~를 질투하는

Jew: a member of the group of people who lived in Israel and believed in Judaism in ancient times 유태인

K

keep: to stay in a state, position, or place without changing or moving 보존하다, 지키다

L

lamentation: words or actions that show that you feel very sad 애통, 애가

leap: to jump into the air 뛰어오르다

leprosy: a serious disease that affects the skin, nerves, and bones and can cause people's fingers and toes to fall off 문둥병, 나병

loyal: willing to support, work for, or be a friend to someone, even in difficult times 충성하는

lyre: an ancient Greek musical instrument with strings and shaped like the letter U 수금 (고대 그리스의 현악기)

M

mortgage: a legal agreement in which you borrow money from a bank in order to buy a house or land 저당, 담보

multiply: to increase something by a large amount 늘려주다

N

nickname: an informal name that your friends or family call you that is not your real name 별명

not A(,) but B: B instead of A A가 아니라 B

notorious: famous for something bad 악명 높은

nurse: a woman whose job is to look after a young child 유모

O

obey: to do what a law or a person says that you must do 복종하다, 따르다

offend: to make someone upset and angry by doing or saying something 모욕하다, 화나게 하다

official: someone with an important position in an organization 관리

on someone's side: if you are on someone's side, you support them in an argument or a fight ~의 편인

order: to tell someone to do something, or to say that something should be done, in a way that shows you have authority 명령하다

orphan: a child whose parents have died 고아

overcome: to succeed in dealing with or controlling a problem 극복하다

overhear: to hear what people are saying during a conversation that you are not involved in 엿듣다

overturn: to turn upside down 뒤집다

owe: to need to give someone back money that they have lent you 빚지다

P

pagan: relating to an ancient religion that had many gods and praised nature 이교도의

part: to move apart 갈라지다

permission: the right to do something that is given to you by someone in authority 허락

persecute: to treat someone extremely badly, or to refuse them equal rights, especially because of their race, religion, or political beliefs 박해하다

persuade: to make someone agree to do something by giving them reasons why they should 설득하다

Philistine: a member of a race of people who lived in Palestine 블레셋 사람

pitiful: looking or sounding so unhappy that you feel sympathy and sadness 가련한

plot: a secret plan to do something bad 음모

plow: to turn over the soil before putting seeds into it 밭을 갈다

point out: to tell someone something 지적하다

preach: to talk about a religious subject at a religious meeting, especially in church 복음을 전하다, 설교하다

priest: a man who performs religious duties 사제, 성직자

prime minister: the political leader in some countries 수상

proclaim: to state or announce something publicly 선언하다, 선포하다

pronounce: to formally state an official opinion or decision 선언하다

property: things, especially valuable things, that are owned by someone 재산

prophesy: to describe a future event using religious or magic powers 예언하다

prosperous: rich and successful 부유한

protect: to keep someone or something safe from harm, injury, damage, or loss 보호하다

put A into B: to move A into B, especially using your hands A를 B에 넣다

R

raven: a large bird with shiny black feathers 큰부리까마귀

refuse to do: to say you will not do something that someone has asked you to do ~하기를 거부하다

reign: if a king or queen reigns, they officially rule a country 다스리다, 통치하다

reject: to not agree to an offer, proposal, or request 거절하다

relationship: the way in which two or more people or things are connected with or involve each other 관계

relearn: to gain knowledge or experience of something again 다시 배우다

repair: to fix something that is broken or damaged 고치다, 수리하다

repent: to recognize that you have done something wrong and to feel ashamed and sorry about it 회개하다, 참회하다

repentance: the act of showing that you feel ashamed and sorry because you recognize that you have done something wrong, especially against the rules of your religion 회개, 참회

report: to provide information about something that exists or has happened 보고하다, 신고하다

request: an act of asking for something in a polite or formal way 요청, 부탁

restore: to make someone or something start being in a particular situation again 회복시키다

revere: to have a lot of respect and admiration for someone or something 존경하다, 우러러 공경하다, 경외하다

revive: to make someone become conscious or alive again 소생시키다

riches: expensive possessions and large amounts of money 부

righteous: morally good or correct, especially according to standards set by religion 정의로운

roam: to move or travel with no particular purpose 배회하다

royal: relating to a king or queen or the members of their family 왕가의, 왕족의

run away from: to leave a place, especially secretly, in order to escape from someone or something ~에서 도망치다

S

salvation: the act of being saved by God from evil 구원

scared: frightened, or worried 무서워하는, 두려워하는

seek to do: to try to do something ~하려고 애쓰다, 노력하다

send: to arrange for someone to go to a place to do a job 보내다

separation: a period of time that people who are usually together spend apart 분리, 헤어짐

shepherd: a man whose job is to take care of sheep 양치기

sign: something that suggests that a good or bad thing will happen in the future 징후, 징표

sin (n.): an action, thought, or way of behaving that is wrong according to religious laws 죄

sin (v.): to do something that is wrong according to religious rules 죄를 짓다

slave: someone who is forced to work very hard for someone else 노예

sling: a piece of rope or leather used in the past as a weapon for throwing stones 투석기, 물매

soothe: to make someone more calm and more relaxed when they are feeling nervous, worried, or upset 달래다, 위로하다

sore: a small painful area of skin that is injured or infected 종기

spare someone's life: to not kill someone, even though other people are being killed ~의 목숨을 살려주다

spit out: to force something such as food or drink out from your mouth 뱉다

stall: a narrow space for an animal 외양간

steal: to move somewhere quietly and secretly 몰래 빠내다

stream: a small narrow river 개울

survive: to stay alive despite an injury, illness, war etc 생존하다

swallow: to make food or drink go from your mouth down through your throat and into your stomach 삼키다

T

tactic: a particular method or plan for achieving something 책략

take away: to remove something 빼앗다

take someone's place: to do something instead of someone else 대신하다

teachings: the ideas or principles of a religious, political, or moral system of a particular person or group 가르침

tempt: to try to persuade someone to do something wrong by offering them a reward if they do it 유혹하다

the needy: poor people 궁핍한 사람들

the poor: poor people 가난한 사람들

the rich: rich people 부유한 사람들

third: in the place or position counted as number 3 세 번째의

threaten: to tell someone that you might or you will cause them harm, especially in order to make them do something 위협하다

throne: the position of being a king or queen 왕위

tithe: a tax that people paid to the church in the past 십일조

torment: to make someone suffer severe physical or mental pain, often deliberately 고통을 주다

treasure: a very valuable and important object such as a painting or ancient document 보물

turn away from: to refuse to accept or to use something any longer ~을 멀리하다

U

unite: if people, groups, or countries unite, they join together, often to work together to achieve a particular goal 통일하다

unjust: not fair or reasonable 공정하지 않은, 정의롭지 않은

V

valley: a low area of land between mountains or hills 계곡

vast: extremely large 어마어마한

verse: a small group of sentences in the Bible 절

vicious: extremely unkind or unpleasant 사악한

W

wake up: to stop sleeping 잠에서 깨다, 일어나다

warn: to tell someone that they will be punished or that something bad will happen if they do something 경고하다

warning: an action or statement telling someone of a possible problem or danger 경고

warrior: a soldier, especially in the past 용사, 군인

wave: to move something around in the air 흔들다

weapon: an object that can be used to hurt people or damage property, for example a gun, knife, or bomb 무기

weep: to cry because you feel unhappy or have some other strong emotion 울다

widow: a woman whose husband has died and who has not married again 과부

wisdom: good sense and judgment, based especially on your experience of life 지혜

wise: a wise person is able to make good choices and decisions because they have a lot of experience 지혜로운

withdraw: if you withdraw a threat, offer, request etc, you say that you no longer will do what you said 철회하다

witness: to be present when something important happens 목격하다

worship: to feel or show respect and love for a god 숭배하다, 경배하다

worship practice: the activity of showing respect and love for a god 예배, 찬양

MEMO

MEMO

Ten Commandments

1. You shall have no other gods but Me.

2. Do not treat anything else as God.

3. You shall not use the name of the Lord to swear or curse.

4. You shall keep the Sabbath Day holy.

5. Honour your father and your mother.

6. You shall not commit murder.

7. You shall not commit adultery.

8. You shall not steal.

9. You shall not lie.

10. Do not long for other people's things.

(Exod. 20:3-17)